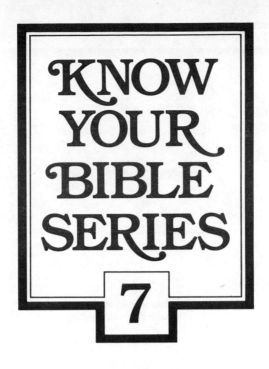

KNOW YOUR BIBLE SERIES

7

PROVERBS
JOB
ECCLESIASTES
SONG OF SOLOMON
PSALMS

D0064300

ROY L. SMITH

ABINGDON PRESS
NASHVILLE

Proverbs, Job, Ecclesiastes,
Song of Solomon, Psalms

INTRODUCTION

With this study we come to the close of our survey of the Old Testament, and the student who has followed the course through to this point finds one great fact standing out above all others: *the Jewish scriptures were a product of the spiritual experience of the nation,* rather than the private writings of a few spiritually minded individuals who shut themselves away from life and who wrote in the privacy of their own prayer closets.

In the Old Testament we can trace the course of economic revolutions and upheavals as serious and transforming in their time as the Industrial Revolution was in the eighteenth and nineteenth centuries of English and American history. The political crises through which the Jews passed were as terrifying in their way and as sinister in their threats as anything the modern world faces, although statistically speaking, of course, the populations involved were almost infinitesimal in their proportions. Sennacherib and Nebuchadrezzar, in their days, were as monstrous as Adolf Hitler in our own.

Out of those awful, direful years devout people spoke while the Spirit of the Most High was upon them; and because they spoke words of divine truth, their messages have a certain timelessness which makes them as useful in our generation as when they were originally spoken, providing we are able to interpret them aright. The words those ancient writers put down with such passionate earnestness were designed to guide the people in their public and private decisions, in their politics and their personal devotions. As we understand the tumultuous conditions out of which they were born we discover the truths they contain and are able to apply them to the tumultuous conditions in the midst of which we live. Their inspiration is proved, not by the manner in which the original writers came into possession of their messages, but by the way those messages are capable of resolving difficulties in any generation when applied to the facts of contemporary life.

They most truly read the Bible who read it with the largest understanding of the earth-shaking struggles out of which it came. They are most inspired by reading it who are most familiar with the spiritual forces which struggled for mastery in the day when the Scriptures were taking form. The truths contained in the Bible will mean most to that student who has

3

the most comprehensive and accurate familiarity with the divergent factors which entered into its composition; and these factors—just as in our own day—will include economics, politics, social ethics, traditions, and racial customs, as well as those things which are traditionally "religious."

One of the most impressive facts which comes to light as we make a fearless study of the Bible is the wide variety of personalities and the large number of individuals who were engaged in producing the book for us. No one can know, for instance, how many devout souls of the prophetic party contributed their thought, their convictions, and their moral judgments to the compilation of the Book of the Law which was discovered in Josiah's day (621 B.C.). Neither can anyone know how many devout scholars, working under the guidance of the Spirit of God, labored on the Book of the Law which was finally made the constitution of the Jews by Ezra's proclamation (400 B.C.). But without those patient and pious scholars, saints, and scribes our Old Testament—and our Bible—would never have come into our hands so richly laden with truths mined from the will of God.

It has been said on many occasions that the Jews had a genius for religion, and that is a simple statement of a great fact. No other race of antiquity ever thought more deeply or more accurately on spiritual problems than did the children of Israel. Among them were those who explored the field of faith in every direction and came back to the people with rich treasures. Proverbs and Ecclesiastes indicate that some of their thinkers were far from orthodox, and the fact that these books have been incorporated into the sacred writings is at least a comment on the catholicity of the Hebrew mind.

But it is in the Psalms that we discover the real souls of the plain people. This ancient devotional book, designed to serve the same purpose as a modern book of devotions, put the great spiritual literature of the race within the reach of those humble people upon the street. It aimed to stimulate the piety of the average person; and so successful was the effort that to this day plain people turn to the Psalms for comfort, consolation, restoration, and refreshment. They restore our souls.

ROY L. SMITH

4

Jewish Wit, Wisdom, and Worship

1 What part of the Old Testament do we study in this inquiry?

We will make an investigation of two distinct types of Hebrew literature which are found in the Old Testament. First of all we will study the "wisdom" literature of the Jews, and after that we will make a more or less detailed study of their poetry as it has been preserved for us in the Old Testament.

2 What is the wisdom literature?

That wisdom literature which we find in the Old Testament consists of three books—Proverbs, Job, and Ecclesiastes. These three do not, by any means, constitute all such literature produced by the ancient Jews. There must have been much more scattered about among the people, but these are the only books that have been preserved for us in the Old Testament.

3 Why is it called wisdom literature?

The word "wisdom" had a distinctive meaning when used by the Jew, both in Old and in New Testament times. It meant something similar to our word "philosophy," and may have been equivalent to "common sense," though not all of us would agree that all the sayings of the wise Jews were so sensible. There is a trace of secularism in the wisdom of the Old Testament writers whom we are to study, and in one case at least—Ecclesiastes—the author comes dangerously near to agnosticism. But in general it may be said that Hebrew "wisdom" meant "that common sense which enables a person to live a happy and successful life."

From the earliest times there had been thoughtful persons among the Hebrews who took a great interest in wisdom, just as there are many moderns who are deeply interested in philosophical problems. Such were not peculiar to the Hebrew race, of course, for persons with similar interests and talents were to be found among the Babylonians, Egyptians, and Edomites. Indeed, the wise ones of Edom enjoyed a consider-

5

able reputation throughout the East (Obadiah 8); and at least a section of the book of Proverbs is known to have been taken, at least in part, from Egyptian writings (22:17–23:14). Among the Hebrews, however, the wisdom literature was produced by a class of teachers who made the study of ethics, manners, morals, and worldly wisdom their chief interest and were called "wise men."

4 Were they the same as the "wise men" who came to seek Jesus?

The "wise men" of the New Testament (Matthew 2:1 ff.) who came seeking the young child Jesus seem to have been astrologers from Persia. Scholars are not quite sure of the exact nature of their status and calling, but certainly they are not to be confused with the wise ones who wrote the Old Testament books we are to study. Among the Greeks those Old Testament thinkers might have been called philosophers, and perhaps among the people of today they might be rated as psychologists. They were not distinctly religious except as they were interested in studying problems related to religion, or as they were concerned with an investigation of the teachings of religion.

5 Were they a professional class?

So far as we know they did not earn their livings by their teachings. Rather they were people of native shrewdness, wide observation, and a high moral sense, who believed they had found the secret of a happy and honorable life and sought to teach this secret to their contemporaries. In a sense they may be called the successors of the prophets, for they spoke their mind as teachers of the people, voicing the truth as they saw it.

6 Were they real prophets?

Apparently they did not call themselves such, and at least two of the great prophets held them in a certain contempt (Isaiah 5:21; 10:13; 28:9; 29:14; 31:2; Jeremiah 4:22; 8:8 f.; 9:23; 18:18). They reported no visions, organized no political party, religious movement, or social group, and seemed content to play the role of teachers of the common people. Only seldom did they claim any divine sanction for the things they taught. Rather they depended upon the truth they uttered to vindicate itself and make its own appeal to the good judgment of those who heard.

For the most part they dealt with the profound moral and philosophical problems with which the human mind has always been engaged when it has been thoughtful.

7 Who were some of these "wise men"?

Unlike the prophets, many of whom have left their names to us, these people did not usually succeed in making their own names permanent, and we have but three. In the book of Proverbs there is a collection of sayings attributed to Agur (30:1), another collection of sayings attributed to King Lemuel (31:1), and two collections which are said to have come from King Solomon (10:1; 25:1).

8 Who were Agur and Lemuel?

No one knows. Their names do not appear anywhere in the Old Testament outside of the book of Proverbs. It is impossible to state anything more precise than that they were men who achieved some temporary fame among the Jews as coiners of epigrams and proverbs.

9 What about Solomon and the Proverbs?

The opening verse of the book of Proverbs credits the composition to King Solomon, son of David (1:1), as a result of which the entire collection is commonly called "Solomon's Proverbs"; but the book says of itself, very definitely, that it is a series of collections (1:1; 25:1; 30:1; 31:1). Moreover, it is known to be a fact that at least one rather considerable section is derived from Egyptian writings (22:17–23:14) which have been taken from a book that may date back as early as 1000 B.C. Solomon is said to have composed proverbs (I Kings 4:32), but it seems safest to accept the book of Proverbs as a collection of the sayings of the wise of Judah which have accumulated through the long years of the nation's history. Just as David is credited with having written the Psalms, many of which we know were written by others, so Solomon has been mistakenly credited with having written all the book of Proverbs.

10 Is this not rather disconcerting?

It should not be, for we are only allowing the Bible to speak for itself and tell its own story. The most reverent thing we can do is to read the Bible and allow it to speak for itself and believe what it really says about itself. If the book of Psalms, for instance, says that numerous authors are represented by the poems of which it is composed, then the most reverent and respectful—also honest—thing we can do is to take it at its word and learn all we can about all the authors mentioned. It is at this very point that we discover the difference between a truly scientific study of the Bible and one that is primarily interested in preserving some ancient tradition or interpretation. The scientific study seeks for the facts, establishes them as facts, and then allows them to speak for themselves.

11 What about Solomon's proverbs?

There is good historical evidence to indicate that Solomon was greatly interested in wisdom and that he did compose proverbs and songs. The editor of the book of Kings, probably the most dependable historian in the Old Testament, describes him as having produced three thousand proverbs having to do with nature subjects—cedars, hyssop, beasts, fowls, creeping things, and fishes (I Kings 4:32-34). In the book of Proverbs, however, there are but thirty-eight verses of this type; and, curiously enough, thirteen of these are to be found among the sixty-four verses of the last two chapters, these being credited to Agur and Lemuel. If it is true that Solomon's proverbs had chiefly to do with nature subjects, it would seem that we have comparatively few from his hand left to us. The most reasonable judgment in the case seems to be that Solomon was greatly interested in this type of learning and literature, that he gave it great encouagement, that it developed under his sponsorship into a definite type, that he produced some himself, and that he bequeathed his name to the type of literature without actually composing much of it. This seems to be about as much as we really need to know.

12 What about the Egyptian section of Proverbs?

Jewish scholars and thinkers, from the days of the Exile forward, were at least somewhat familiar with the contents of the literature of other nations of the East. Archaeologists know that an Egyptian book called "The Wisdom of Amen-em-ope" did exist, and are familiar with its contents, which were contained in thirty chapters, the composition being dated sometimes between 1000 and 600 B.C. Ten of the twelve sayings of Proverbs 22:17–23:14 are very clearly adapted from this Egyptian source; and the last of the series of twelve (23:12-14) is taken, with some slight modification, from another Egyptian book known as "The Sayings of Ahikar," fragments of which have been found among papyri discovered at the ancient island of Elephantine.

13 What may we conclude, then, about Proverbs?

It seems to be a collection of collections, consisting of at least eight different groups of sayings in epigrammatic and poetical form, coming from the witty, the wise, and the thoughtful philosophers among the Jews following the destruction of the kingdom of Judah. Particular sayings may have originated in some form far back in the history of the nation and been incorporated into some collection at a much later date.

14 Which is the first collection?

It includes the first nine chapters of the book of Proverbs, and is divided into two sections: (a) The first six verses of the first chapter are not, strictly speaking, proverbs, but a lengthy and incomplete sentence which may be read as the official title of the book, or as an introduction which attempts to define the material the readers will meet as they proceed. (b) The second section (1:7–9:18) is an address in which a wise father—wisdom personified—addresses his son on the subject of religion. He calls it "the fear of Yahweh" and extols its blessing (2:1-11, 20-22). The youth is warned against wicked men (2:12-15; 3:27–4:27; 6:1-19) and women of easy virtue (2:16-19; 5:1-19; 6:20–7:27).

15 What is the second collection?

The second collection (10:1–22:16) is easily identified as a separate group by its subtitle (10:1). It consists exclusively of brief maxims comprising only a single line of Hebrew poetry divided into two equal parts, several of which are repetitions, in full or in part, of other proverbs (e.g., 14:12; 16:25).

16 What is the third collection?

The third grouping, which includes the Egyptian section, is

called "the words of the wise" (22:17–24:22) and consists of advice to young men who are entering upon their careers as public officials. Besides some counsel on personal matters, such as etiquette and morals, there is sound admonition concerning religion. The second section of the collection (23:15–24:22) warns against the grosser sins of drunkenness and adultery, and more subtle offenses like envy and malicious joy in the misfortunes of enemies. Criminals condemned to death are to be treated humanely, and the religious note is sounded in the assurance that God sees the hidden thoughts (24:12, 18).

17 What about the fourth collection?

This brief section (24:23-34) is really a supplement to the preceding one and is a mixed group which offers, among other things, a picture of the sluggard's field (24:30-34).

18 What about the fifth collection?

This, according to the subtitle (25:1), is another collection of "proverbs of Solomon" (25–29). The first section is largely secular (25–27), but the second has a strong ethical and religious flavor with a marked emphasis upon the Jewish doctrine of retribution (28–29). It will be noticed that a number of the proverbs of the second collection are repeated in the fifth in one form or another.

19 What was that doctrine of retribution?

As was explained in Study No. 6, it was a fixed belief of the Chronicler that piety brought prosperity and that sin resulted in misfortune, and that book was written for the purpose of proving that theory. It was a doctrine that originated in the teachings of the prophets, but it came to its full fruitage in the work of the great teachers of the Law.

20 What about the sixth collection?

Here we come upon an entirely different sort of material, in "The words of Agur son of Jakeh of Massa" (chap. 30). The author is unable to understand God and his administration of the universe (30:1-4), but for the most part the comments are secular in character.

21 What about the seventh collection?

"The words of Lemuel, king of Massa" (a desert tribe which lived between Edom and Arabia) profess to be the teachings of the king's mother (31:1-9), who warned her son against sensuality and intoxication and urged him to deal justly with the poor.

22 What about the eighth collection?

This superb poem (31:10-31) has been called the best of its kind in all the Old Testament. It is an acrostic poem (in which each line begins with a letter of the Hebrew alphabet in order) describing an ideal wife and mother. In the Septuagint she is called "an intelligent woman," but in the Hebrew Old Testament, "a woman who fears Yahweh" (31:30), which introduces the religious element much more conspicuously.

23 What about the wisdom of the wisdom literature?

So far as the book of Proverbs is concerned, there are two distinct philosophies of life expressed. One might be called the secular interpretation of life, for it teaches that the good life is to be attained by diligence, frugality, knowledge, and decency. The other believes that prosperity, long life, and other good fortune are an immediate reward bestowed upon the righteous in compensation for their obedience and faithfulness. The prophets often took the position that wisdom had nothing to do with religion and even regarded it, at times, as antagonistic to religion in spite of its high moral standards. Much of the book of Proverbs deals with human affairs from the humanistic angle without regard to any religious sentiment or conviction. There is no spirit of social daring or politicial reform in the book, though honor, justice, fair dealings, and righteousness are commended many times. On the whole, however, the advice of the book is that of expediency—it is better to be good because evil does not pay. This is the doctrine of retribution in a slightly different form.

24 When was the book of Proverbs compiled?

There is no way of knowing precisely, though it is easy enough to fix the date somewhere between 400 and 200 B.C. It is positively known to have been in existence in 200 B.C.; and various references to the Law (28:4, 9; 29:18), combined with other evidence, make it impossible before the day of Nehemiah. Good scholarship seems to sanction a date somewhere about 300 B.C.

25 In what form did the writers compose?

They were poets of a sort, composing their sayings in the form of a verse or couplet of two parallel members in which two things were compared to bring out their likeness, their contrast, or some comparative difference. Occasionally they composed in three, four, or even five lines. Very rarely do we find poems of greater length, though the longer poem known as "Wisdom's Soliloquy" in chapter 8 and the poem on the ideal woman in the last chapter of the book are exceptions to this rule.

26 What was their religious viewpoint?

They were Jewish, of course, but they always addressed their readers—or hearers—as human individuals rather than as Jews. They have very little to say about the ceremonial laws, less about Jewish religious doctrines, and still less about anything that could be called theological. They seem to think of wisdom as something universal, and their rules of life as being applicable to life everywhere. They used the name "Yahweh," but if we would substitute the simple word "God," we would find their maxims as pertinent in our lives as they were in theirs. They believed that goodness was always rewarded and that wickedness was always punished, and their advice as a consequence is always based on self-interest. They may be called highly moral without being highly idealistic. They taught how to live sagaciously rather than piously; they were shrewd without being devout.

27 What about the book of Job?

Like the book of Jonah, which is written *about* a prophet rather than *by* a prophet, the book of Job is an exquisite poem written *about* one of the ancient worthies of the Hebrew race and not *by* him.

28 What does this mean?

It means that the author of Job was a great thinker who put

12

the ideas down in poetical form, using the name of Job as a literary device, but being content to remain anonymous. It means, too, that the book does not profess to be history, but is very frankly literary. It is to be read, therefore, as a piece of literature—profoundly thoughtful—and not as a piece of factual reporting.

29 What sort of literature is it?

It is a very remarkable bit of dramatic poetry which introduces at least four major characters and some lesser ones, designed to present a discussion of one of the most profound themes with which the mind ever deals.

30 What is that theme?

It can be very simply stated, but it would require at least a small library to answer it: *Why is it that people suffer?* The Jews had an answer for the question, but it did not satisfy this greater thinker, whom we shall assume was a man, and he set out to find one that would be more satisfactory.

31 What was the Jews' answer?

As has been described in other studies in this series (Chronicles, Samuel, Kings, etc.), the Jews believed in the doctrine of retribution. This doctrine taught that good fortune always follows righteous living and bad fortune always follows wickedness. The wise ones who composed the sayings found in the book of Proverbs believed in this doctrine very definitely, and it may be said to have been accepted generally by the Jews. But the author of Job had seen enough of life to know that it was not wholly true; he had seen good people suffer, and he had seen some wicked persons prosper greatly, all of which convinced him that there must be a more satisfactory explanation of life.

32 Why call Job a poem?

Because that is exaclty what it is in the original Hebrew. The King James Version does not reveal its poetical form, but this has been corrected in the Revised Standard Version and other modern translations. For this reason it is recommended that the student use one of these in this study.

33 How does the book rank as poetry?

Tennyson called it "the greatest poem of ancient or modern times," and Thomas Carlyle "one of the grandest things ever written with the pen. . . . There is nothing written, I think, in the Bible or out of it of equal literary merit." By common agreement it is the greatest poetical work of the Bible and is entitled to take its place alongside the masterpieces of literature produced in any language.

34 Who was Job?

According to the book of Job he was a devout and pious man (1–2; 42:7-17) who lived at some early period of Hebrew history. There is a single reference to such a man in the book of Ezekiel (14:14, 20) which describes him as a more or less vague personality like Noah or one of the early patriarchs. Apparently there was some story concerning him current among the Hebrews of that day which has not been preserved to us, but which was picked up by the author and used as a vehicle for presenting the truths he wished to teach. Whether Job was actually a historical person or not makes no difference so far as the truth or merit of the book is concerned. Its teachings are altogether independent of the question of the identity or historicity of Job as a person.

35 When was the book of Job written?

The story of Job, a devout man who suffered many trials and tribulations in spite of his piety, and who remained faithful to God until he finally triumphed, is evidently one that had been told among the Hebrews for hundreds of years. Then came a profound thinker who, studying the story and the facts of life, asked himself a staggering question: Why did this good man suffer so undeservedly when he had been righteous? Various answers occurred to him, each of which was held by some party, or favored by some logic, but each of which was also unsatisfactory. Finally, perhaps for the sake of expressing his own ideas on the subject, he wrote his thoughts down and gave his book to the world. But he makes no allusions to any historical event or person which might afford us a clue that would enable us to discover the time when he did his work;

and, unfortunately for us, no other writer of ancient times has made any reference to his book. The result is that we are unable to decide on any date except in the most general terms. We know that the book of Job appeared in early editions of the Septuagint version of the Bible, and that fixes it previous to 200 B.C. Careful scholars think it could not have been composed earlier than 500 B.C.; so the best we can say is that it was written somewhere in that three-hundred-year period. For that matter, an exact date probably makes less difference in the case of the book of Job than in the case of any other writing.

36 Why does it make so little difference?

Because its opinions and conclusions are, actually, timeless. The problem it discusses is moral and not historical, and the solution of a moral problem does not depend upon a historical date.

37 Why is Job counted as a part of the wisdom literature?

It is true that it is not written in the literary style of Proverbs. Also, so far as we know, it was not written by one of the wise ones of the Jews. But it is an outgrowth of the principle accepted by the wise ones which declared that piety produced prosperity. It is a magnificent effort on the part of a philosophical mind to solve that problem. Because it represents the effort of a great thinker to explain the administration of the universe in terms of God, it has been called wisdom literature and is accepted as such.

38 Is the book religious?

The book is profoundly religious, but it deals with the question of religion in a way that is altogether unique and different from anything else in the Bible. No Jewish laws, customs, religious institutions, practices, rituals, or ceremonies are referred to in any way. There is no mention of the Temple, of any altar, priest, prophet, law, or sacred book. Nowhere is there any exhortation to prayer; nowhere is there any call to repentance. It is a book with a strictly personal appeal, and yet nowhere does the author preach to his readers as if he were trying to persuade them to a way of life or thought. Perhaps one

15

of the most peculiar facts about the book is its unusual use of names for God. All this indicates that the author of the book was a layperson, unconnected with the professional religious classes or organizations.

39 What unusual names does the author of Job use for God?

In all other Old Testament books the usual names for God are "Yahweh" ("Lord") and "Elohim" ("God"). But in Job these names are rather rare. True, they appear often in the prose prologue and epilogue (1:1–2:13; 42: 7-17), but there is reason to believe this material was quoted from (or else added by) some other writer. In the poetry "Yahweh" is used only three times in God's speeches (38:1; 40:1) and twice in Job's replies to them (40:3; 42:1)—another occurrence (12:9) is probably an interpolation—and "Elohim" appears at only six scattered places (5:8; 20:29; 28:23; 32:2; 34:9; 38:7). Instead we find three other names: "El" fifty-five times, "Eloah" forty-one, and "Shaddai" thirty-one.

40 Are these names used elsewhere in the Old Testament?

"El" is regularly used for "god" uncapitalized (as in Deuteronomy 32:12), and in compounds and phrases for "God" capitalized (as in Genesis 14:18). Occasionally, it stands alone and means "God" (Psalm 19:1; Isaiah 14:18; etc.). "Eloah" is a less common word for "god" and is used a few times to mean "God" (Psalms 50:22; 139:19; Proverbs 30:5; etc.). 'Shaddai," translated "the Almighty," appears several times (Ruth 1:20; Psalm 91:1; etc.). But outside of Job these names are all exceptions.

41 Why are they used so much in Job?

First of all, it was probably an effort to avoid monotony. But some scholars are of the opinion that the author of the book may have been an Edomite, using Edomite names, or that he may have drawn upon the thinking of some Edomite. The names of Job's friends are not Jewish names, a fact which lends support to this theory. Edomite wise ones enjoyed a considerable reputation (Obadiah 8), and any literature they may have had would become current among the Jews very easily, for the languages of the two races were similar.

42 Did any foreign literature get into the Bible?

We have already learned that a section of the book of Proverbs is of Egyptian origin (22:17–23:14). Agur (Proverbs 30) and Lemuel (Proverbs 31:1-9) were non-Jewish; and at least two psalms (88; 89) are by non-Hebrew sages (I Kings 4:31), while another (104) is thought by some to be a paraphrase of an Egyptian song.

43 What about the contents of the book of Job?

There are six major divisions in the book, each of which is composed of minor sections, as follows:
1. The story in prose—1:1–2:10; 42:10b-17
2. The dialogue
   a) Introduction—2:11-13
   b) Job's bitter speech—chapter 3
   c) The first cycle of speeches—chaps. 4–14
      (1) Eliphaz labors with Job—chaps. 4–5
      (2) Job's pathetic reply—chaps. 6–7
      (3) Bildad's speech of assurance—chap. 8
      (4) Job's reply, commenting on God's character—chaps. 9–10
      (5) Zophar enters the argument with an assertion of Job's sin of which he is unconscious—chap. 11
      (6) Job answers Zophar and defends himself—chaps. 12–14
   d) The second cycle of speeches—chaps. 15–21
      (1) Eliphaz speaks again, rebuking Job—chap. 15
      (2) Job appeals to God for vindication—chaps. 16–17
      (3) Bildad returns to the fray, picturing the godless—chap. 18
      (4) Job's reply describes his wretchedness and prophesies his further vindiction—chap. 19
      (5) Zophar speaks again, asserting that the wicked are only temporary—chap. 20
      (6) Job replies to Zophar, calling attention to the fact that some wicked people prosper all their lives—chap. 21
   e) The third cycle of speeches—chaps. 22–27. This section

17

e) is somewhat confused, and there may be some question about our reconstruction, but the following seems to be reasonable.

(1) The third speech of Eliphaz attempts to point out Job's sins—chap. 22

(2) Job answers Eliphaz, declaring God's administration is incomprehensible—chaps. 23–24

(3) Bildad asserts the certainty of punishment for the wicked—25:1; 27:7-10, 16-23

(4) Job answers Bildad once more, offering to teach his friends something about the nature of God—26:1-4; 27:11 f.; 25:2-6; 26:5-14

(5) The third speech of Zophar describes the lot of the wicked—27:13; 24:21-24, 18-20; 27:14 f.

(6) Job continues to assert his innocence in the face of his affliction—27:1-6

f) The epilogue, in which Yahweh rebukes the friends and restores Job's fortunes—42:7-10a

3. The poem on wisdom—chap. 28

4. Job's soliloquies—chaps. 29–31

a) Job's former happiness—chap. 29

b) His present misery—chap. 30

c) His high ethical and moral standards—chap. 31

5. The speeches of Elihu—chaps. 32–37

a) Prose introduction, bringing in Elihu, the younger man—32:1-5

b) Elihu's first speech, in which he apologizes for his youth and exhorts Job to listen to God—32:6-22

c) Elihu's second speech, accusing Job of blasphemy—chap. 34

d) Elihu's third speech, which declares God is too great to be affected by man's actions or desires—chap. 35

e) Elihu's fourth speech, in defense of God's administration of justice—chaps. 36–37

6. The speeches of Yahweh—chaps. 38–41

a) The amazing fact of the inanimate world—38:1-38

b) The equally amazing animal world—38:39–39:30

c) Yahweh challenges Job to explain it all—40:1-2, 6-14

d) Job is reminded of the hippopotamus and crocodile—40:15–41:34

e) Job's replies, in which he admits that he spoke without an adequate understanding—40:3-5; 42:1-6

44 What is the argument of the book?

It was the accepted belief of the Jews that the righteous are rewarded and that the wicked are punished, all according to their deeds. The book of Job challenges this theory of life and undertakes to study the problem anew, by means of a series of speeches and arguments. The book is not a dialogue, but a series of statements in which the different theories of life are set forth. Upon the foundation of the ancient story of Job the whole structure is built.

45 What was that ancient story?

There was a man who had lived righteously all his life and had prospered. But Yahweh and Satan fell to discussing him one day, and Satan declared that if he were to suffer he would forsake all his piety and become as others. A test was agreed to, in which Satan was allowed to afflict Job in any way he pleased with only one restriction—he must not take his life. Thereupon one disaster after another befell him until he was bereft of fortune, family, and health. At last, when his misery had mounted to its climax, he was called upon by three friends who came to comfort him. So great was his misery that he cursed the day of his birth (3:1 ff.), and with that the argument between the friends of Job gets under way. According to the ancient story, quite probably, the story ended with Job's fortunes restored and "everybody happy."

46 What did the author add to the story?

Scholars seem to think that the author took this ancient story of a pious man who prospered, suffered, and was restored, and added the arguments and various philosophies, making the story a vehicle for carrying his ideas.

47 About what did the debate revolve?

About the cause of Job's misery. What is the reason for such unhappiness and misery? Each one of the three friends takes up the question, and to each Job makes reply. When the friends have nothing left to say, Job renews his complaint and is answered by Yahweh.

48   What is the attitude of the friends?

The three friends all believe in the popular doctrine that suffering is due to sin; but, since the life of Job has been so far above question, they are under the necessity of finding some other explanation. First of all, Eliphaz speaks (chaps. 4–5)

49   What does Eliphaz have to say?

He rebukes Job rather mildly and reminds him that God is bound to visit retribution on the sinful. He exhorts him to penitence and assures him that he will be delivered and, ultimately, rewarded. This was the usual solution—"You are suffering, of course, but it must be because you are a sinner. Therefore, if you will repent, all will come out right and you will be rewarded in the final count."

50   How does Job react to this?

He declares that his friends have deceived him like a brook that has gone dry (6:14-23), and that their comfort is a bitter disappointment. His pain is so terrible that he is justified in his complaint (7:1 ff.), and he begs God to leave him alone (7:11-21). Then follows Bildad.

51   What does Bildad have to offer?

The second friend offers no more satisfaction. God, he says, is just (8:1-4) and would bless Job if he could, but evidently Job does not deserve it (8:5-22). There must be some sin of which he is not aware.

52   What is Job's reaction to this charge?

He admits that no one is perfect (9:1-3), but God does not seem to be governed by the same moral standards which prevail among humans (9:4-13), and Job is therefore helpless (9:14-21). He can expect neither mercy nor justice from God and is therefore in despair. Why doesn't God let him die and end it all (9:22–10:22)? It is the voice of cynicism and despair. But one more friend is still to be heard from.

53   Who is this third friend, and what does he have to say?

Zophar assures Job that God cannot be deceived, and that the sin of which he is guilty will come out. Let Job therefore throw himself on the mercy of God, for his wisdom is beyond their power to understand. If he will do so, then he will be safe (chap. 11). It is the voice of one who advises blind, unreasoning trust in God in spite of the facts.

54   What is Job's reaction to Zophar's speech?

The sufferer asserts that he is as wise as his friends and that he sees all they see. He is well aware of the fact that he must live somehow in God's world (12:1-25). They have all shown themselves poor advocates for God, and Job is not afraid to present his case directly to the Most High (13:1-19), providing he can be assured that he will not be annihilated for his temerity (13:20-22). He challenges God to indict him (13:23). Then he launches out in a cynical discussion of life in which he declares there is no hope for a person who dies (14:7-12), for death is the end (14:16-22).

55   Does this end the matter?

It only marks the beginning of a second cycle of speeches in which each friend adds new comments and Job answers them.

56   What is Eliphaz' second speech?

He rebukes Job for his brazen attitude toward God and assures him that pain is the portion of the wicked from time immemorial (chap. 15).

57   What is Job's reaction?

He has heard all this before and is tired of mere "words" (16:3). In fact, he wishes he might change places with his friends and comfort them for a time (16:4 f.). With this he turns to God and calls upon him to witness in his behalf that he is innocent of sin. At the same time he declares that his only hope is the solace of death (16:6–17:16).

58   What is Bildad's second speech?

He refuses to listen to Job's pessimism and lack of faith (18:1-4) and depicts a dreadful future for the godless (18:5-21).

59   What is Job's reply to this?

He reproaches his friends, asserts that he has been unjustly afflicted, and declares that the future will vindicate him and even God will admit that he has been wronged (chap. 19).

60 What is Zophar's second speech?

He uses the old argument that the triumph of the wicked is but temporary, and that they will eventually suffer (chap. 20).

61 Does Job have any answer for this?

He disproves the doctrine by showing that some of the wicked have prospered all their lives, and that they have never suffered misfortune. This argument is therefore without foundation (chap. 21).

62 Have the three friends ended their appeals?

No, they return to the debate, each one speaking and each one receiving a reply from Job (chaps. 22–27).

63 What is the substance of Eliphaz' third speech?

Eliphaz makes another attempt to prove Job's sinfulness, and to show that he deserves his misfortune, but assures Job that he can still avoid greater disaster by turning to God (chap. 22).

64 How does Job meet him this time?

He declares he would like to appear in God's court and there defend himself, but that court cannot be found. He cannot understand why God has hidden himself from the pious; his administration of human affairs is incomprehensible. Evil is everywhere, and no one can deny it (chaps. 23–24).

65 What is the substance of Bildad's third speech?

He is very sure that prosperity will save no one from divine punishment (25:1; 27:7-10, 16-23).

66 How does Job reply to this?

He indulges in a bit of sarcasm (26:1-4) and proposes to instruct his friends concerning the nature of God (27:11 f.; 25:2-6; 26:5-14).

67 What is the substance of Zophar's third speech?

He closes the dialogue with a description of the "portion of a wicked man" as ultimate death, disaster, and ruin (27:13; 24:21-24, 18-20; 27:14 f.).

68 What is Job's final answer?

In spite of all the punishment he has suffered, Job maintains his innocence (27:1-6).

69 Is this the end of the story?

Several remarkable chapters follow, including the poem on wisdom (28), Job's monologues (29–31), and the speeches of Elihu (32–37), besides four speeches of Yahweh and a reply by Job. But the basic story upon which the book is founded probably ended with this last dialogue, and the epilogue perhaps should be read at this point in order to get the original tale.

70 What is the epilogue?

Having heard all the speeches, Yahweh reproves the friends, restores Job's fortunes, and all is well again (42:7-10a). From this point on, the rest of the book is something in the nature of an appended comment.

71 What is the poem on wisdom?

By many this is esteemed to be the most perfect piece of Hebrew poetry in the Old Testament. The piece has five stanzas consisting of a refrain followed by five verses. (1) Minerals lie in the earth, but (2) though miners are able to reach them, (3) wisdom is not to be found there nor (4) can it be purchased. (5) Only through God can it be found. (chap. 28.)

72 What about Job's monologues?

There are three of them, all dealing with Job's problem (29–31): (1) A description of Job's former happiness and good fortune. (2) He is now held in derision, and calamity is his lot. (3) Yet he has conquered sensuality in his own life, has treated all people fairly, including his servants, has been upright in his thinking, hospitable and just.

73 What about Elihu's speeches?

A young man now enters the argument, evidently confident

that he can answer Job where the older men have failed. Neither Job nor his three friends answer the youth, as in the previous debate, and he proceeds to make four speeches (32–37).

74 What does he say in his first speech?

He opens with a courteous statement to the older men, but is confident that he has some inspiration they do not have. Since they have not been able to answer Job, he can no longer keep silence. He then takes up the lament of Job, and begins to answer his charge that God does not speak to them by saying that God does speak through dreams, illnesses, and warnings. Therefore Job should listen (chaps. 32–33).

75 What does he say in his second speech?

He charges Job with blasphemy for having accused God of dealing unjustly with him (chap. 34).

76 What is Elihu's third speech?

Job had argued that neither sin nor piety meant anything to Yahweh (35:1-3), and Elihu argues that God is too exalted to be affected by human actions, but that the doer suffers all consequences. People cry in vain only because they lack true faith, and for this reason God has been deaf to Job's cry (chap. 35).

77 What is the substance of the fourth speech?

Elihu is determined to defend God's good name and his justice. True, if the sinner will not repent, God is helpless; but God uses affliction to increase one's faith. Certainly those who cannot explain the cataclysms of nature can hardly be expected to explain the nature of God (chaps. 36-37).

78 What about the speeches of Yahweh?

There are four of them, each calculated to make Job realize the inadequacy of his humanity and the beneficence of God's ways: (1) There are the wonders of the inanimate world (38:1-38), and (2) the wonders of the animal world (38:39–39:30). (3) Yahweh next invites Job to answer some simple questions, and the man confesses his inability. This means that he is altogether unequal to meet God on his own level, and is therefore unable to save himself (40:1-14). (4) Then follows the description of the hippopotamus and the crocodile (40:15–41:34), with which no one has ever been a match.

79 What is Job's answer to all this?

He realizes his insignificance and Yahweh's might; he admits that he has spoken hastily and without understanding, and repents (42:1-6).

80 What is the final solution of the problem?

In broad terms the book seems to take the position that the problem is insoluble, like God's other wonders. Job shares the belief that misfortune is the result of sin at the outset of his experience, but once he is afflicted he is sure that the theory is a mistaken one. He does not deny his faults, though he continues to assert his innocence, but at least he believes that to punish him for being what God made him to be is unfair. He is driven to believe that God is arbitrary, unjust, and immoral; but still he cannot give up his confidence in God, for he has long believed him to be righteous. He seems to think of a God of righteousness over against a God of arbitrary cruelty, but he believes in the God of righteousness and struggles to put his trust in him. He is convinced that the God of righteousness will sometime triumph and establish himself. As he realizes that he is not the center of the universe around which everything moves, and takes a humbler attitude, his problem resolves itself somewhat. The problem of suffering is just as insoluble as it ever was, but the very fact that God has appeared to him is sufficient to strengthen his faith, and he is finally convinced that God governs the world righteously, even though his rule appears mysterious. Stated simply, the book of Job offers five answers to the question, Why is evil allowed?

a) It is to test the goodness that is only superficial (Satan).

b) It is to punish wickedness, whether wickedness is recognized by the evildoer or not (the three friends).

c) God is really unjust (Job).

d) It is to warn, educate, and train humanity (Elihu).

e) It is to bring home to them the fact of human ignorance (Yahweh).

25

81 Is the answer satisfactory to modern thought?

One has the feeling that Job has not been able to make up his own mind in the matter, but we have to admit that he has given about all the answers there are. Modern thought has very little additional light to throw on the problem. At least this can be said: the book of Job contains the oldest and the most effective effort the Hebrew mind ever made to deal with the problem and find an answer. Here is a sincerity of mind and a range of thinking that is to be encountered in no other book of the Old Testament.

82 Is the book of Job a book of faith?

The answer to this question will depend in some part upon our definition of faith. True, the faith of Job is not of the same quality as that of the wise ones who wrote Proverbs, nor even such a faith as we find in Amos, Isaiah, Jeremiah, or Habakkuk. Yet there is a religious faith in it that is, in certain respects, higher and finer. Perhaps it can be said that, in some respects, the faith of Job is higher than that of Isaiah, for we have no record of the great prophet's ever having faced up to the intellectual difficulties with which Job dealt. The faith with which Job emerged was a faith that had looked squarely into the face of the worst and ended by believing the best. Certainly Job was far ahead of Proverbs.

83 In what respect?

The sages who wrote Proverbs taught an exalted ethical code and followed the prophets in declaring that God is more pleased with righteousness than with ritual. But, as firm believers in the doctrine of retribution, they always held out the promise of good fortune as the recompense for righteousness. "The reward for humility and fear of Yahweh," they confidently declared, "is riches and honor and life" (Proverbs 22:4). The author of Job, on the other hand, takes the case of a man who has met all the conditions—Job was "blameless and upright, one who feared God, and turned away from evil" (1:1)—and yet, in spite of his admittedly fine morality (29:12-17; 31:1, 5-8, 9-12, 13-15, 29-30, 32) and rare spirituality (1:5, 31:26-27, 24-25), has suffered one calamity after another. He is a complete refutation of the universal validity of the doctrine of retribution.

84 Did Job abandon the doctrine of retribution?

This is exactly why the book was written. In the main argument the author gives half the time to the older view, but all scholars agree that the book was written for the purpose of denying the universal validity of the doctrine. In all Job's addresses he speaks his mind to Yahweh with complete frankness and, at times, almost with brazen effrontery. In no other book of the Old Testament, with the possible exception of Habakkuk, does anyone stand upon moral dignity and dare to answer God as in the book of Job. He takes his position on four points.

85 What is his first point?

He believes the doctrine of retribution is indefensible, because it does not explain all human suffering or happiness. He can see no dependable or universal relationship between prosperity and goodness, or between adversity and wickedness. Moreover, he does not fall back on any promise of happiness after death to compensate for the loss or lack of happiness on this earth. He does seem to have had some glimmering ideas about immorality (7:6-10; 14:7-22; 17:13-16; 19:25-27), but he does not depend upon a future world to correct the mistakes of this one.

86 What is the second point in his position?

Abandoning the doctrine of retribution, Job does not abandon his faith in Yahweh. He is determined to go on believing even after the doctrine has been shown to be inadequate.

87 What is the third point in his position?

He has a confidence in Yahweh so great that he is sure God will not be offended by honest doubts. God, he believes, will honor honesty from his creatures and welcome from them a frank declaration of their difficulties. Here is a "charter of free speech in the presence of the Almighty."

88 What is the fourth point in his position?

Job stoutly maintains his innocence, believing that nothing is

27

to be gained in confessing a sin where no sin exists. He does not believe in any "original sin" that calls for any "atonement"; neither does he see any need for reconciliation between himself and God, for he is conscious of no wrongdoing. In all this he is far ahead of the author of Ecclesiastes.

89 What is Ecclesiastes?

It is the third in the group of three books which compose the wisdom literature of the Old Testament.

90 Who wrote Ecclesiastes?

It is impossible to identify the author of the book as any particular individual, for he has hidden behind an assumed name, "Koheleth." The Greeks translated it Ecclesiastes, but in English it means "one who addresses an assembly or a congregation," and this has been abbreviated to "Preacher." Again, we assume the author is a man.

91 Does the book mention no author?

It is said that he had been a king in Jerusalem (1:1, 12), and the first verse identifies him as "the son of David" (1:1). The book of Kings (I Kings 8:1) tells of Solomon's assembling the elders of the nation, and this may have suggested that he was a "koheleth." But there seem to be good reasons for believing that Solomon was not actually the author of the book.

92 What are those reasons?

Some of the statements made in the book could hardly have come from Solomon. He would not have been apt, for instance, to boast that he was wiser than his father (1:16). He would hardly have paid honor to the second born (4:15) since he was not one such. Or, again, he would not have advised resistance to authority (10:4 ff.). In another case the author is identified, not as a king, but as a preacher who collected and composed many proverbs (12:9-11). The young reader is actually advised not to read the book (12:12 f.), advice which Solomon could hardly have been expected to offer.

93 Why should Solomon's name be connected with the book, then?

It was a literary custom of the time to attach the name of some great historical personage to a writing, partly for the purpose of gaining a hearing for its message, and partly for the purpose of lending importance to the utterances. In this case it was fortunate for the book that this was done, for the attachment of the name of Solomon to it probably saved it from oblivion and secured for it a place in the Old Testament. As a matter of fact, considerable argument revolved about the book for many years, and it won its place in the canon over stubborn resistance.

94 When was the book written?

There is no date mentioned inside the book itself, and any judgment in the matter must be based on (1) the language used in its composition, (2) references to the book in other writings of a known date, and (3) the ideas with which the book deals. Taking all these factors into consideration, it seems safe to say that it was composed about 200 B.C.

95 With what does the book deal?

It might be well to call it a book on "The Meaning of Life" for it was not only with the problem of pain that the author dealt, but with the whole problem of life itself. He wanted to know what the significance of life may be, what there is in life that is really worth living for, what the central good and goal of life may be, and what there is in life in which one may believe without being deceived.

96 How does the author proceed?

The book consists of a series of discourses somewhat after the style of the book of Job, except that Ecclesiastes does not have any clear-cut sequence or order. One speech does not depend upon another. Rather the book is a collection of observations and meditations set down more or less at random, as might be done by someone who undertook to state conclusions concerning life, writing a little one day, adding a little on another day, and still more on a later occasion, without ever returning to the task to arrange the material according to a logical plan.

97 What is Koheleth's first observation?

He has watched human life and the operations of nature and

has come to the conclusion that life has neither goal nor meaning. The sun rises and sets, only to go back over the process again and again. One generation follows another and is succeeded by still another; the wind blows and returns the next day; the rivers run into the sea day after day without filling it. All is ceaseless struggle that gets nowhere, and for which there is no meaning (1:8-9). "All is vanity," he declares (1:2).

98 Did he see no good in life?

He felt a powerful inner urge of some sort which drove him to seek knowledge (1:13), but the more he knew the sadder he became, for even the pursuit of knowledge was hopeless and unrewarding (1:18). He tried pleasure, business, activity, and entertainment, but they were equally empty (2:1-9). Neither wisdom (1:18) nor success (2:11) provided any satisfaction, for one black, threatening, sinister fact stands at the end of the line.

99 What is that fact?

The fact of death! He was comforted with no beautiful hope of immortality, nor stirred with any thought of a life of achievement in another world. He was in all respects a man of this world.

100 Did he give up?

No, he did not grow completely cynical and advise suicide. Instead he continued to believe there was some good in life (11:7) and that "a living dog is better than a dead lion" (9:4). More powerful than his disillusionment was his instinctive love of life; so he continued in his search for wisdom in the belief that knowledge was better than ignorance (2:13), and went on working for the sake of the pleasure it gave him (2:10). But though he might have admitted that these small rewards were pleasurable, he was perfectly sure that neither wisdom, wealth, nor work was the true and chief aim of life, for the sage and the fool meet the same fate; one cannot take wealth away with one, (2:18 ff.) and one may not have the capacity for enjoyment even though one has honors and riches (6:1 ff.).

101 What was his conclusion?

He seems to have come to the conclusion that the world was

in such utter confusion that there was no principle by which it could be explained (9:11). People are not rewarded according to their deserts, and there is no good reason, so far as he can see, to believe that God rules righteously. There is a certain Epicurean emphasis on fate (chap. 1 and elsewhere), and so far as the facts of life are concerned he cannot decide whether God loves the human race or not (3:16, 4:1; 8:16–9:1). Nor is there any moral government worthy of respect in this world (5:8 f.; 7:15; 8:14), and the greatest riddle of all is the fact of death with which we are all confronted ultimately (9:2 ff.). Though some might hope for immortality, Koheleth entertained no such solace (8:7, 3:19 f.).

102 Was he not religious?

He may have believed that the universe was created by some Divine Power, but that Power was not, to him, a loving personality, a kindly creator, or even an approachable divinity. He was a spiritual dictator to whom humans did not have access, a ruler who could not be understood, a tyrant who could not be moved. Koheleth did not deny the existence of God; he only refused to believe he had any moral character.

103 Did he have no solution?

He believed that in spite of the fact that God could not be understood, we must go on asking questions and seeking knowledge (3:10 f.; 11:5). We are living in a world we cannot change (3:1 f., 14; 7:13), but there is no use worrying (3:9; 7:14). Therefore let us take life as we find it and make the best of it, for there is no escape except by death, which is even more hopeless than life (2:24; see also 3:12 f., 22; 5:18; 8:15; 11:7-10).

104 Is he utterly hopeless?

This is one of the strange things about the book—no matter where the author's reason led him, his faith brought him back to something reassuring. He has found enough of goodness in life that he offers youth one of the most exalted bits of advice to be found in all the Old Testament (11:9–12:8), wherein work and joy are to be combined and out of them will come the satisfactions of life. But in nothing is one to be too serious, for it does not pay (7:16-18).

105 Does he advise abandon?

By no means. Koheleth was no sensualist, nor was he immoral. In spite of his skepticism he believed that the good life was preferable to a wicked life, and the chaste life better than that of the libertine.

106 Was he irreligious?

The total impression of the book is one of skepticism, but the author did believe that life had come from the hand of God (3:13, 22; 5:19); and though God was not personal to him, he had no ridicule for those to whom he was. On the contrary, he insisted upon reverence and sincerity in performing religious rites (5:1-6).

107 What is the religious value of the book?

Judged by Christian standards it is of small value. Perhaps the best we can say for the author is that he faced life frankly, judged it relentlessly, and earns a measure of respect by his intellectual honesty. But the perplexed soul will find small comfort in it, and the bewildered will find no solution for their problems in it. The one admirable quality about it is the fact that Koheleth's faith survived the inability of his intellect to carry him through to a dependable basis of logic and fact. But, even so, we have one other book which is of even less religious value.

108 What book is of less religious value than Ecclesiastes?

A tiny little book of poems, of eight short chapters, entitled "The Song of Solomon" in the Revised Standard Version, as in its predecessors, but called "The Song of Songs" by many modern scholars.

109 What is the difference?

The opening verse of the book identifies it as "The Song of Songs, which is Solomon's" (1.1). In Hebrew the expression "song of songs" is meant to express the superlative, as "holy of holies" meant the most holy place of all. This verse undertakes to say that this book of verse is the most beautiful of all the 1,005 songs which Solomon is reported to have composed (I Kings

4:32). But, as in the case of Proverbs and Ecclesiastes, there is very grave doubt as to whether or not Solomon had anything to do with the actual composition of the book except to lend his name as sponsor. Almost the only reason for assigning the name of Solomon to these ancient poems is the frequent use of his name (1:1, 5; 3:7, 9, 11:8; 8:11 f.). But, for that matter, it makes no difference who wrote the songs, for their character remains the same.

110 What is the Song of Songs?

It is a collection of love poems which are supposed to be sung at a wedding feast by the bridegroom, the bride, and their friends. Nine in all, they are perfect illustrations of the "popular" songs of the rural Jews of the period of 300-250 B.C.

111 Which is the first poem?

The couple is married as the poem opens (1:2-8), and the bride sings for her beloved and apologizes to her ladies for her dark skin (1:5)! Verses 7 and 8 may possibly recall a first meeting of the shepherd girl and her rural lover.

112 Which is the second poem?

It consists of a duet between the bride and groom (1:9–2:7), in which the man sings of his beloved's beauties and she responds in similar vein (1:9-11, 12-14). There follows an animated exchange, and finally the girl pleads that her lover shall take her to a tavern (2:4-6).

113 Which is the third poem?

The bride has certain lovely memories (2:8–3:5) of her lover singing to her. She dreams that she misses him, and after finding him she takes him to her mother's house.

114 What is the fourth poem?

It is a highly descriptive report of a rural wedding (3:6-11).

115 What is the fifth poem?

The young man sings a passionate description of his beloved (4:1-7) and of his love (4:3-11), whom he compares to a garden (4:12–5:1).

116   What is the sixth poem?

This poem seems to be a report of a dream. One night after the maiden has retired she hears a knock at the door, but when she goes to admit her lover he has vanished (5:2–6:3). When she goes out to search for him she experiences various misfortunes, whereupon she pleads with her girlfriends to take a message to him, whom she describes with great affection (5:8-16), and when they ask where he may be found, she sends them to his garden.

117   What is the seventh poem?

This is an intimate poetical description of the bride's beauty (6:4–7:9). She is dancing, and as she sings and dances the guests sing of her beauty, beginning with her feet and moving up her body to her head, as might have been expected when a girl was dancing. The poem closes with a passionate expression of love (7:6-9).

118   What is the eighth poem?

It is another song of the bride (7:10–8:4), in which she expresses her desire to tramp the countryside with her beloved (7:10-13) and voices the wish that he were her brother so that she could kiss him in public without shame or embarrassment (8:1-4).

119   What is the ninth poem?

It is not, strictly speaking, a poem but a collection of songs and fragments (8:5-14). There is the maiden's eloquent description of the passion of love (8:6 f.). As a child she had been protected, but this was unnecessary for her very charms protected her (8:8-10). The poem closes with an ecstasy from the lover, who declares that with such a bride he does not envy even Solomon and his great wealth and wisdom (8:11 f.).

120   Are these not very frank poems?

It should be noted that, in spite of a certain frankness in recounting the story of physical charms and caresses which is somewhat shocking to Western ears, the symbolism which is so prominent in the poems is an Oriental effort to express reserve. Symbols such as lilies (2:2), gold (5:11), doves (4:1), etc., do not

34

yield suggestions of the physical body, even though they may have had that meaning to the original hearers.

121 What can be said of the entire collection?

It is very likely that the various poems have come from various authors, though the same theme runs through them all. It is an anthology of rural love songs. The poems deal with the thrills, delights, torments, and fascination of love between a man and a woman; and with their Palestinian background and springtime setting they make a group as exquisite as they are intimate. There is a freedom of action in the poems—as when the lovers appear on the street together (8:1-4)—which was not characteristic of the East generally and indicates that they are imaginative scenes rather than actual descriptions. But the absence of all religious allusion and sentiment make the book one of the strangest in the Old Testament.

122 How did it get into the canon?

In the first place, the impression that it came from the pen of Solomon carried great weight. Then it became the custom to interpret it allegorically, a practice which began as far back as the first century A.D. There were Jewish scholars who declared it was an idealization of Yahweh's love for Israel. Among the Christians there were those who professed to find in it an allegory of the love of Christ for his Church. It is possible, of course, to find such analogies, but the book was not originally wirtten for the purpose of setting forth any such ideas. It is simply a collection of secular love songs, in contrast to the book of Psalms.

123 What about the book of Psalms?

This is a collection of 150 poems, preserved for us in the Old Testament, wherein is to be found a representation of the inner spiritual life of the Jews revealed in its most beautiful and inspiring form. It is, in fact, five books combined in one.

124 Why speak of five books in one?

Because that is exactly what it is. In the Revised Standard Version of the Bible the student will find the five divisions plainly marked. It even happens in an occasional edition of the

King James Version that the subdivisions are noted, though no mention was made of any such in the original edition of 1611.

125 What are the five divisions?

Book I—Psalms 1–41
Book II—Psalms 42–72
Book II—Psalms 73–89
Book IV—Psalms 90–106
Book V—Psalms 107–150

126 How can these divisions be identified?

Four doxologies are introduced very plainly (41:13; 72:18 f.; 89:52; 106:48), and the last psalm of the collection (150) is a doxology for the entire collection.

127 When were these divisions first made?

The student must be careful to avoid confusion at this point. The divisions were not *made* by the translators of the book of Psalms. They only *recognized* them. The original arrangement of five books was a part of the plan of the original compilers, and the translators only reproduced in English what the editors and compilers of the book of Psalms provided for in the original Hebrew.

128 Why did they plan five divisions?

As we have already learned, the great Book of the Law had been divided into five books of about equal length for the sake of convenience in handling. Then, in time, this idea of a fivefold division became fixed in the Jewish mind. A very ancient writer had said that "the Hebrews divided their Psalter into five books so that it would be another Pentateuch."

129 Why call the book of Psalms the "Psalter"?

The English name "Psalms" comes from a Greek word which meant the playing of a stringed instrument and the music produced by such playing. The original Hebrew title simply meant "praises." Thus the Greek title described its form and the Hebrew title its contents. But in one manuscript of the Greek Septuagint translation (Codex Alexandrinus) the word *psalter-ion*—meaning the stringed instrument ("psaltery" in the King

James translation of Psalm 150:3, etc.) itself—was used as the title; and from this word the English form "Psalter" became popular.

130 Are the psalms strictly religious songs?

It can almost be said that the book of Psalms contains only religious poems, but one psalm (45) is in praise of a royal couple on their wedding day, and has no religious significance. A few of the compositions do not seem to have been designed for singing (34:11-22; 37; 49; 73; 127; 128; 133) but are called "wisdom poems." Then there are at least three (19:7-14; 112; 119) which are tributes to the Law. On the whole, however, the title of the book indicates that the entire collection was thought of as songs of worship which were to be sung to the accompaniment of stringed instruments.

131 What kind of stringed instruments did they have?

Psalm 150 lists a considerable number of musical instruments in common use among the Jews, all of which seem to have been used in connection with musical portions of the Temple services.

132 What do we know about ancient Jewish music?

Little or nothing. They evidently had tunes of some kind, for at least two are mentioned in the book of Psalms, but what those melodies may have been we do not know. There is no record of any scale, staff, or other musical form. Whether they had yet invented harmony we do not know. Their poetry indicates that they had a marked sense of rhythm, and this probably made for metrical forms, but this must remain only a surmise. There are, however, a few musical terms still preserved in the book of Psalms which indicate that some form of music was rather well developed—sufficiently so that titles and headings in the book of Psalms could indicate the musical terms with an assurance that the reader would know what was expected of the singers.

133 What were some of these musical terms?

They fall into two groups: (1) those which define the character of the psalm, (2) those which indicate the purpose of the psalm. Then there were (3) instructions concerning certain ritualistic acts and (4) strictly musical terms.

134 What about the character definitions?

There is some question about the exact meanings of some of the technical terms used in connection with the psalms, and not all scholars would agree, perhaps, with all the precise definitions suggested in this and the following paragraphs; but they seem to represent the best opinion among careful students.

The term *mizmor* (3 and others) is used in the title and is translated "psalm," but it means a song accompanied by a musical instrument. *Shir* ordinarily means a secular as well as a religious song, but in the book of Psalms it is used to describe only "a religious song" (18; 46). There is an entire group of psalms (120–134) with the title *Shir hamma' aloth*, translated "A Song of Ascents," which were designed to be sung by the people when they escorted the sacred ark in the festal parades.

Miktam is the title given to several psalms (16; 56–60) which were sung in connection with services organized about the idea of atoning for sins. These were always individual songs rather than congregational hymns. *Maskil* is the title for a song accompanied by music which is considered to be the result of the special spiritual insight of a seer, priest, prophet, or Temple singers (32; 42; etc.) *Shiggaion* is a term applied to a lamentation hymn (7) and probably refers to some ritualistic act performed during the singing. *Tehilla* is translated as "song of praise" (145) and *tephilla* as a "prayer" (90, etc.).

135 What about the titles indicating purpose?

Lethodha in at least one instance means "an expression of thanks" accompanying an offering (100). *Leannoth* means "penitence" (88) and was probably composed as a "prayer of confession." *Lehazkir* means "bringing sins to remembrance" (38; 70) and many refer either to the sins of the psalmist (Leviticus 5:12) or to the acts of some enemy from which he is suffering. *Jeduthun* simply means "confession" (39; 62; 77)—it was mistaken by the Chronicler for a person's name—and refers to a penitential attitude of mind and heart. *Lelammedh*, translated "for instruction," refers to a worshiper who has been inspired by Yahweh (60).

136 What about the ritualistic instructions?

The term *lamenacceah* is used in connection with fifty-five psalms (beginning with 4), and is translated "to the choirmaster" or the like; but recent scholars have suggested that it means, "to put God into a gracious attitude." In one psalm (56) *jonah elem rehokim* used in the title may mean "concerning the dove for far-away gods." In connection with one of the ceremonies a dove was released and was supposed to fly away to the far-off gods with the guilt of the worshiper. Evil spirits were supposed to cause misfortune and illness (Leviticus 1:14; 5:6-10; Zechariah 5:11), and the dove was supposed to put these enemies into good humor again. *Aijeleth hash-shahar* may in the title of Psalm 22 refer to the sacrifice of a ewe as a sin offering at the break of day (Job 1:5), this psalm being sung by the priests and the worshiper at such a time.

Shoshannim in the titles of Psalms 45 and 69, *shushan eduth* in the title of 60, and *shoshannim eduth* in the title of 80 are variants of the same phrase meaning "concerning lilies of the ark" (Exodus 30:36; Numbers 17:10) and may refer to their use in the ceremonial. Leviticus 23:40 states that branches of beautiful trees were to be carried up to the Temple and placed around the altar. Perhaps flowers were laid before the ark as this song was being sung. *Mahalath* (53; 88) probably indicates songs to be sung in connection with purification after an illness. *Alamoth* (46) may refer to a liturgical act, of which playing on a harp was a part, in the autumn festival. *Sheminith* in the title of two psalms (6; 12) may be the last act in the ritual of purification. *Gittith* (8; 81; 84) means "over the winepresses" and seems to have been associated with the harvest festival in some way which is not quite clear.

137 What about the musical terms?

There are at least two classes of these—one appearing in the titles and one in the body of the psalms. *Neginoth*, translated "stringed instruments" (6; 54; 55; 67), indicates that a certain ritualistic act was performed to the accompaniment of music, somewhat as the administration of the elements of the holy communion might be accompanied by singing. The expressions *higgaion* and *selah* appear in various psalms (9:16; 61:4; and variously elsewhere) and probably mean about the same thing. The world *selah* means "lift up" and in the psalms probably means that the congregation was to lift up the cry, "For his steadfast love endures for ever." It might be about like "amen" in some modern liturgies.

138 Were the psalms used in public worship?

It is a little difficult to know just how the psalms originated, for the history of all could not have been the same. In some instances a public worship hymn became a private hymn used in personal devotions, and in other cases the private hymn passed over into the public worship. The Chronicler (I and II Chronicles) makes much of the Temple singers, and their part in the public services was very considerable. It is very probable that many songs originated with them, just as modern music originates with professional musicians and is taken over by the public. However they may have originated, however, we know that psalms constituted an important element in the services of public worship.

139 How were they used in public worship?

Some may have been recited in concert and others chanted. some were sung antiphonally, and others as anthems, while still others were sung as is the modern hymn. In numerous instances a solo voice was used with responses in something of the fashion of a certain type of modern Negro spiritual. Numerous psalms were designed to be sung with musical accompaniment as we use hymns with an organ accompaniment. Numerous directions appear in the book of Psalms indicating that certain hymns are to be used for special services and occasions.

140 What about the hymns for special occasions?

Psalm 30 was to be used at the Festival of the Dedication of the Temple. Psalm 100 was to be sung with the thank offering. From the Septuagint and other sources it is learned that each day in the week had a special psalm—24 for Sunday, 48 for Monday, 82 for Tuesday, 94 for Wednesday, 81 for Thursday, 93 for Friday, and two, 38 and 92, on the Sabbath. Psalm 29 was sung during the last two days of the Feast of the Tabernacles, 39 and 81 on

New Year's Day, and 113–118 were sung during the slaying of the pascal lamb, with parts of these psalms also sung during the Feast of the Tabernacles. Much of the responsibility for all this fell, of course, upon the guilds of Temple singers.

141 What were the singing guilds?

The origins of the Temple music are shrouded in considerable mystery. The first direct knowledge we have of the singing guilds appears in Nehemiah's memoirs (11:17; 12:24), when three such are mentioned. In Ezekiel's plans for the restored Temple elaborate provisions were made for accommodating the Temple musicians (Ezekiel 40–44), and it is known that the exiles were familiar with some Temple songs (Psalm 137:3-4) during the early years of their exile (beginning 586 B.C.). Some authorities believe that Nahum used great choirs of priests in anthems, chants, and hymns in connection with his pageant celebrating the fall of Nineveh in 612 B.C., but it is not until the period of 400 to about 250 B.C. that the Temple music was organized under the direction of bands of singers officially designated for that responsibility.

142 What does that indicate?

It means that the Jewish hymnals took form during this period and the psalms as we have them in our Old Testament were collected. The regular use of hymns in connection with the Temple music is referred to by the Chronicler (I Chronicles 16:8 ff.) about 250 B.C., when the Levites sang Psalms 105:1-15 and 96:1b-13a, concluding with a doxology (106:1) to which the congregation responded (106:47 f.).

143 How did the singing guilds originate?

Concerning this matter we have little information. We do know that the three Levitical guilds of Temple singers were considered to be descended from Asaph, Jeduthun (sometimes called Ethan), and Heman, who are said to have been placed in charge of the Temple music by David (I Chronicles 15:17, 19; 25:1, 6). At one time the guild of Asaph seems to have been the only one (Ezra 2:41; Nehemiah 7:44; 11:22; 12:45), but at least two guilds—Korah and Asaph—are represented in the book of Psalms by collections of songs.

144 Who were the Korahites?

Korah was the name of an Edomite clan (Genesis 36:5, 14, 16, 18; I Chronicles 1:35) which became a part of the tribe of Judah during the period of the wilderness wanderings. At first they refused to recognize the special priestly function of the Levites (Numbers 16) but later became a Levitical group (Numbers 26:9-11). They began their religious career as cooks (I Chronicles 9:31) and gatekeepers (I Chronicles 9:19; 26:19), but eventually became Temple singers (II Chronicles 20:19) and developed their own collection of psalms (42–49; 84; 85; 87; 88). Another guild, known as the guild of Heman, seems to have merged with them (I Chronicles 6:33-37), and Psalm 88 is attributed to each group. By the year 250 B.C. they seem to have become one of the old and honored groups of Temple musicians.

145 Who were the Asaphites?

They were the oldest of the three guilds. According to the Chronicler (II Chronicles 29:30) Asaph was a seer who lived in the time of David and Solomon and was recognized as the chief of the singers (Nehemiah 12:46; I Chronicles 15:17, 19; 16:5; II Chronicles 5:12). This guild likewise seems to have developed its own collection of hymns.

146 When were the psalms written?

Poetry is one of the oldest forms of literary expression, and numerous poems are to be found in the Old Testament outside the book of Psalms which are entitled to a place in the book so far as literary quality, spiritual passion, and poetical form are concerned. In Exodus 15:21 we have the song of Miriam, which probably comes from the time of Moses (1290 B.C., or perhaps even a hundred years earlier). The fifth chapter of Judges is a poem, much in the style of a psalm, which celebrates a victory over the Canaanites. Second Samuel 23:1-7 is another such selection.

Hosea 6:1-3 and 14:1 ff. are songs that were to be sung, and Isaiah 2:1-4 (very similar to Micah 4:1-3) bears a strong resemblance to Psalm 122. Amos 6:5-6 perhaps makes reference to the sacrificial songs of the shrines, and Isaiah 30:39 seems to refer to psalms used in connection with the Temple feasts. In Joel (1:8-14), Jeremiah (14:7-9; 16:19 f.; 17:7 f.), Habakkuk (chap.

3), Isaiah (38:10-20), and First Samuel (2:1-10) we find material very similar to poems in the book of Psalms. All this indicates that the people were accustomed to psalms at an early date, and it is highly probable that at least some of the psalms go back to the earliest years of the nation, perhaps in primitive form.

Following the destruction of Jerusalem (586 B.C.) numerous psalms seem to have been produced. Mention has already been made of the fact that the exiles were familiar with their ancient Temple songs (Psalm 137:3-4). In addition, Second Isaiah includes six psalms of great literary and spiritual merit (40:12-31; 42:10-12; 44:23; 49:13; 52:9; 54:1-10). In Third Isaiah we find three more (61:10 f.; 63:7–64:12; 66:10-14). In the book of Jonah we find at least one short psalm (2:2-9), and Isaiah 25:1–26:10 is a psalm from the early Greek period, sometime perhaps about 331 B.C.. The Chronicler credits a psalm to David (I Chronicles 29:10-19) and puts prayers upon the lips of Ezra, Nehemiah, and the Levites (Ezra 9:5-15; Nehemiah 1:5-11; 9:6-37).

147 What does all this prove?

It proves that through a thousand years of Hebrew history the people were producing religious songs of one form and another, and that the psalms we have in the book of Psalms have probably come from all that period. Some may have originated in a single couplet, like Miriam's song, and been elaborated with the passing of the years. Others may have been born full-orbed out of a given situation. But the date in each case must be determined by the subject matter of the psalm itself.

148 Is it possible to date any of them exactly?

In the case of at least one (137), it seems quite evident that it came out of the early years of the Exile, for it reflects clearly the sad memories of that experience, as well as a vivid hatred for the oppressors. Three other psalms (74; 79; 83) seem to have come out of the Maccabean period of Hebrew history (subsequent to 185 B.C.), for no other fits so well the conditions mentioned in the psalms. Aside from these we cannot be sure.

149 Who wrote the psalms?

All but thirty-four of the psalms bear some sort of title, the exceptions being called "orphan psalms" by the Jews; but it must be remembered that the titles were no part of the original composition. Just when the titles became attached to the psalms no one knows, though some of them do represent very ancient traditions. But we have an important and valuable method for checking on the matter. The Greek translation of the Hebrew Old Testament which is called the Septuagint (about 250 B.C.) carries titles for many of the psalms which were evidently taken from the text with which the Greek translators worked. The Massoretic text on the other hand—the Old Testament that has come down by way of the Hebrew—also has many titles attached to the psalms. These can be compared. In some cases they agree, but in other cases there is variation. Even so, the exact meaning of many titles has been lost as they have come down through the years. This means that it is very difficult to know for a certainty who the original authors may have been.

150 Did not David write many of them?

We know that David was a musician (I Samuel 16:14 ff.) and that he wrote some poetry (II Samuel 1:17 ff.; 3:33 ff.). The titles credit David with the authorship of seventy-three, but some of these bear internal evidence that he could not have written them. They deal with religious ideas that David knew nothing of, or they refer to political situations which could not have existed until long after David's death. Then, too, the form of the title raises some questions. "Of" or "belonging to" is used in all cases, which may mean that they were a part of a collection made by David, or made in David's name, or dedicated to David, in which case he may have had little to do with the actual composition. It is very common to hear modern people speak of the "Moody and Sankey" hymns, but no one ever thinks that the two famous evangelists wrote all the hymns so referred to.

151 Are any other names mentioned?

Twelve are attributed to Asaph, nine to the sons of Korah, two to Solomon, one to Heman, one to Moses, and one to Ethan. And it should be said that the Jews commonly believed in 200 B.C. that David, Moses, Asaph, and Solomon had all been composers of hymns.

152 Is the book of Psalms the ancient hymnbook of the Jews?

It has been called "the hymnbook of the Second Temple," and

doubtless much of the material it contains was used in the Temple services; but it cannot be called a hymnbook in the modern sense of the word, for the people did not use books in their Temple services. All their responses, hymns, anthems, and songs were memorized and sung without reference to any book. Rather the book of Psalms was intended as a collection of poems aimed to be of spiritual benefit to the laity, especially the plain people. It was an anthology of religious poems prepared for a specific religious purpose.

153 What was that religious purpose?

During the period of the Babylonian Exile a movement got under way among the exiles which terminated in the announcement of the Book of the Law as the governing constitution of the people. This movement undertook to stimulate piety among the Jews and combined patriotism and religious fervor. The pious person believed that being personally pious was serving the nation. With the proclamation of the Book of the Law as the constitution of the Jews this "pious movement" began to lay great emphasis upon the holy character of the Law. The pious esteemed the Law much as the modern Christian exalts the gospel. It became the object of their affection and the spiritual nucleus around which their devotion centered. As the modern Christian speaks of "love for Christ," the ancient believer exclaimed, "Oh, how I love thy law!" (Psalm 119:97). They believed themselves fortunate indeed in the fact that they possessed the Law (1:2; 19:7; 37:31; 40:8; 78:5, 10; 94:12; etc.), and this possession was, to them, an evidence of Yahweh's great devotion to Israel (119:165).

The book of Psalms is a collection of religious poetry which was compiled for the purpose of promoting this pious movement among the people. The student who makes a study of the psalms with this fact in mind will discover an entirely new world of meaning. A clear line of demarcation is drawn between the "righteous" and the "sinners," the difference being their attitude toward the Law. This is done in something of the fashion of modern evangelistic literature which speaks of the "converted" and the "unsaved." The righteous were those who undertook to observe the Law as a guide for their daily life, while "sinners" were those who were indifferent. True, there was a deep underlying moral difference, but this was not

45

emphasized. The basic difference was the conflicting attitude toward the Law. Sinners were regarded as outcasts and the righteous as the nation's hope (139:19-22).

154 Does the poetical form appear in the English Old Testament?

At this point it is necessary to make some inquiry into the form and character of Hebrew poetry, and the student must be prepared for the fact that it differs considerably from English poetry. We are accustomed to think of a poem as something that includes rhymes and "stanzas," and in the English form in which most of us have read the psalms these characteristics are lacking. In the first place, if there had been any rhyme in the old Hebrew poetry it would be lost in translation. But Hebrew poetry did not attempt rhymes. Instead, it took another form. This did not appear in the King James Version, but it does appear in the Revised Standard Version.

155 What is the basic principle of Hebrew poetry?

The Hebrew poets undertook to achieve a certain balancing of lines, sometimes called "parallelism." This appears in six distinct forms of poetry, all of which are to be found in the book of Psalms.

156 What is the first form?

The simplest and most common form is called the "distich," or simple couplet, but it appears in four variations. The illustrations we will use for all of the forms have been furnished by Dr. Julius A. Bewer,[1] one of America's most trustworthy scholars, but the translations are from the Revised Standard Version.

a) There is a synonymous parallelism, in which a thought expressed in the first line is duplicated in the second with the words only slightly different, as in Psalm 21:2:

> Thou hast given him his heart's desire,
>   and hast not withheld the request of his lips.

It will be noted that there is no fundamental difference in the meaning of these two lines; the second only adds strength to the first.

46

b) There is a second form, tautological parallelism, in which the same words are exactly, or almost exactly, repeated, as in Psalm 94:3:

> Yahweh, how long shall the wicked,
>   how long shall the wicked exult?

c) Antithetical parallelism is in the same form, but instead of a repetition of the same thought the second line contains a contrasting statement, as in Psalm 30:5:

> Weeping may tarry for the night,
>   but joy comes with the morning.

d) Synthetical parallelism, illustrated by Psalm 3:4, is one in which the second line aims to supplement the first:

> I cry aloud to Yahweh,
>   and he answers me from his holy hill.

157 What is the second form of Hebrew poetry?

This is one which uses the same principle just described, but three lines are used instead of two. The same methods of contrasting ideas, and supplementing them with additional lines, is used in the "tristich," or triplet poetry, of which Psalm 93:3 is one of the best illustrations:

> The floods have lifted up, O Yahweh,
>   the floods have lifted up their voice,
>   the floods lift up their roaring.

158 What is the third form of Hebrew poetry?

This consists of four lines, and is very frequently little more than a combination of two distichs, though it is called a "tetrastich." Psalm 55:21 furnishes an excellent example:

> His speech was smoother than butter,
>   yet war was in his heart;
>   his words were softer than oil,
>   yet they were drawn swords.

159 What is the fourth form?

That is, as the student has perhaps guessed, a combination of five lines—perhaps a distich and a tristich—expressing one

---

[1]*The Literature of the Old Testament in Its Historical Development*, pp. 344f. Used by permission of the publisher, Columbia University Press.

47

basic idea. Psalm 6:6-7 is one of the best illustrations:

> I am weary with my moaning;
>   every night I flood my bed with tears;
>   I drench my couch with my weeping.
> My eye wastes away because of grief,
>   it grows weak because of all my foes.

160 What is the fifth form?

The hexastich (a combination of six lines) may consist of three distichs or two tristichs, but in any event the six lines converge upon one idea. Psalm 99:1-3 furnishes an illustration of this form:

> Yahweh reigns; let the peoples tremble!
>   He sits enthroned upon the cherubim; let the earth quake!
> Yahweh is great in Zion;
>   he is exalted over all the peoples.
> Let them praise thy great and terrible name!
>   Holy is he!

161 What is the sixth form?

It is probably the least attractive of all because of its mechanical form, though it seems to have been very popular among the Hebrews. It is called the "acrostic" poem because the successive lines begin with the successive letters of the Hebrew alphabet. If a single line is used for each letter, then the poem is just twenty-two lines long; but some poets preferred to use distichs instead of lines, in which case the poem was forty-four lines in length.

It is easy to see that this mechanical device would become artificial and cumbersome unless it were used with great skill, but in the hands of a clever Hebrew poet it was sometimes very effective. Even among such, however, it was liable to become labored at times, and usually lacked much of the delicacy of the more flexible forms. Psalms 111; 112 are illustrations of the simplest form of twenty-two lines, though of course the use of the Hebrew letters disappears in the process of translation. Three psalms (25; 34; 145) use the acrostic with distichs, and two with tetrastichs (9–10 [originally a single poem]; 37). The most elaborate acrostic poem in the Old Testament is the 119th Psalm, in which the first line of each stanza begins with a successive letter, and this letter is then repeated at the beginning of each of the eight distichs in the stanza.

162 With what subjects do the psalms deal?

In answer to this question we can do no better than quote from Dr. Bewer:

Here the hopes and fears of many ages are collected, the longings and yearnings of countless hearts. Here the penitence and grief over sin, the sorrow and anguish over individual and national calamity, the joyful gratitude for forgiveness and restoration, find voice and utterance. Here the passionate plea for revenge on the enemies individual or national, the despair over the apparent injustice of this world order, and the hope of the coming of God's Kingdom, stand side by side. The whole range of human life, its joy and its woe, its light and its shadow, and its daily routine, is treated in the Psalter. There are psalms of common worship, pilgrim songs and processional hymns, calls to worship, hymns of praise and thanksgiving for individual or national deliverance, for the harvest and the joys of nature. There are national psalms, prayers for deliverance from external or internal foes, for national restoration, prayers of trust in national peril and of praise for past deliverance, battle songs, and odes of victory. There are royal psalms, coronation and wedding odes, prayers for the king's just and ideal rule, for God's help in battle or thanksgiving for victory. There are psalms of individual piety with its longings for communion with God and its joy in the experience of it; with its prayers for help and healing, for forgiveness and purification; with its songs of faith and trust and its hymns of thanksgiving and praise. There are didactic psalms, with the warm, insistent teaching of the fear of God, the divine government in the world, retribution for pious and wicked alike; with their warnings against trust in riches, and concerning the vanity and brevity of life; with their teachings of true worship and true sacrifice, of the blessedness of forgiveness, and of charitableness toward others, of the joys of home and of nature and law; and with their lessons from Israel's great history in the past. Out of the heart of life they sprang, and to the heart they speak. Many poets have contributed; some of them were original geniuses of poetic power, others were common versifiers. They are not grouped according to any chronological, topical, or other principle. Varied as life itself, they are also tossed together in the same kaleidoscopic manner as life's experiences themselves.[2]

163 Are the five books of psalms separate collections?

The five books of psalms mentioned in Question 124 are more or less artificial divisions of the book of Psalms which were intended to divide it to correspond with the Book of the Law.

---

[2]*The Literature of the Old Testament in Its Historical Development*, pp. 340 f. Used by permission of the publisher, Columbia University Press.

But a close observation of the book of Psalms reveals the fact that it does actually include nine separate collections, so that, strictly speaking, the book of Psalms can be called a "collection of collections."

164 Why call it a collection of collections?

As we have already learned, a considerable number of songs had come into existence and more or less common use among the people by the time Ezra appeared in Jerusalem proclaiming the Law as the constitution of the nation. As the services of the Temple grew in dignity and importance, and as the "pious movement" got under way, it seemed important to someone that a collection of these songs should be made for the inspiration of the people and the strengthening of their faith. Making such a collection was a comparatively simple matter, for a number of smaller collections were already in existence, and it was necessary only to bring them together, add a few individual compositions to serve some special purpose, and the book was complete. This is exactly what we have in the book of Psalms.

165 Who did this compiling?

No one knows exactly who perfected the collection, for no record has been preserved. All we can say is that it was done sometime between the time of Ezra and the Maccabean age, when the last psalms were composed which are to be found in the book.

166 What collections were there to begin with?

When the compilers set about to collect the nation's religious songs, they found at least nine great collections already in existence. These they inserted in their collection, usually keeping them in their original form, with their introductions and doxologies.

1. The First Davidic Psalter—2–41
2. The Korah Psalter—42–49
3. The Second Davidic Psalter—51–72
4. The Asaph Psalter—50; 73–83
5. A second Korah collection—84–89
6. A series of hymns—93; 95–100
7. The Hallelujah Psalter—105–107; 111–118; 146–150

8. The Pilgrim Psalter—120–134
9. The Third Davidic Psalter—138–145

167 Do these collections correspond to the five books?

In the case of the first three books the dividing line corresponds to the concluding line of one of the collections. Thus, Book I includes Psalm 1, which is really an introduction for the entire collection, and ends with the First Davidic Psalter. Book II includes the first Korah collection and the Second Davidic Psalter. Book III includes the Asaph Psalter and a second Korah collection. Book IV includes a number of hymns and two of the Hallelujah Psalter. Book V includes thirteen of the Hallelujah psalms and the entire Pilgrim Psalter, the Third Davidic Psalter, and the concluding doxology (150).

168 What about the First Davidic Psalter?

In the opinion of many scholars this is the oldest collection of the entire book of Psalms. How it first came together no one knows, and who compiled it is equally a question. That it has had David's name attached to it for many centuries is a fact, but that David wrote the individual psalms is very doubtful. But there are several facts about the collection in which the student will be greatly interested. In the first place, the name used for Israel's God is "Yahweh" 272 times, and in only 15 cases "Elohim." In the second place, Psalm 14 of the first Davidic collection is much like Psalm 53 of the second Davidic collection, except in two respects. In the third place, three of the psalms (2; 10; 33) have no designation in the Hebrew Bible; but the Greek manuscripts attribute two of them (2 and 33) to David, and make the third a part of Psalm 9.

169 How do the two psalms, 14 and 53, differ?

In our English translations there are seven verses in the fourteenth psalm and six verses in the fifty-third. The student is reminded that neither the verse nor the chapter divisions were any part of the original composition of any part of the Old Testament, but were introduced for the convenience of the modern reader. The fact that in one case the psalm has seven and in the other case six verses is due entirely to the fact that the scholars who arranged the versification did not take the trouble

51

to compare them and make them correspond. This difference between them has no meaning otherwise.

A more significant difference appears, however, in connection with the second variation. Psalm 14 in the King James translation uses the word "LORD," and Psalm 53 uses the word "God." This may seem like a very small matter until we discover that in the original Hebrew the two words were "Yahweh" and "Elohim."

170 What is the significance of that difference?

It might indicate that the two versions of the psalm came from two different sections of the country. It is known, for instance, that the name "Yahweh" was commonly used in the south and that "Elohim" was used in the north. But in the case of the two psalms this becomes especially interesting. Psalm 14 is a part of the first Davidic collection and the name "Yahweh" is used throughout the section. In Psalm 53 the name "Elohim" is used, and we discover that this is true throughout the second Davidic collection. In fact, throughout the second Davidic collection the name "Elohim" is used four times as often as "Yahweh," whereas in the rest of the Psalter the name "Yahweh" occurs almost twenty times as often as "Elohim." This has suggested the name "Elohistic Psalter" for this section of the Psalter.

171 What is the Elohistic Psalter?

It consists of forty-one psalms (42–83) in which the name of "Elohim" occurs very frequently, and includes the second Davidic collection (51–72), the hymnbook of the sons of Korah (42–49), and the psalms of the Asaph (50; 73–83). This is all of Book II and part of Book III, the remaining portion of Book III consisting of a psalm of David (86), four psalms of Korah (84; 85; 87; 88), and a psalm of Ethan (89). Many scholars believe that the first Davidic collection (3–41, 2 being added afterward) is the oldest and first of the Jewish collections and that Books II and III were later additions. There is a possibility that the first Davidic collection was compiled in the south, and that the second collection came together under northern auspices, or that the editor and compiler deliberately changed the name "Yahweh" to "Elohim" to suit their purpose better.

172 Would this have been honest?

At least it was perfectly legitimate. The psalms were not considered scripture, but only religious songs and poems in common use among the people. Anyone who used one of them was at perfect liberty to change them to suit the purpose if so desired. It is a very common thing for editors of modern hymnbooks to change a line, a word, or a phrase of a hymn for some reason. No one thinks it is dishonest; for the hymns are the common property of all Christians, and if by changing a word or a line one can improve it or make it express one's experience more accurately, one feels one has a right to do so, and no one feels anything dishonest has been done. This was the status of the psalms among the Jews previous to their acceptance as a part of the "sacred scripture," which did not occur until after 250 B.C.

173 What does all this prove?

That the hymns were in use long before they became scripture and that in such use they were changed here and there to suit the mood of different singers. It also means that the discovery of the fact that they were "inspired" was made by the people who used them and came under their spell. The duplications that appear here and there indicate that the different collections were made in different sections of the country, or perhaps by different individuals who were certainly not the original authors.

174 Are there many duplications?

Mention has already been made of the case of Psalms 14 and 53. In addition, Psalm 40:13-17 is almost an exact equivalent of Psalm 70, and Psalm 57:7-11 added to Psalm 60:5-12 equals Psalm 108. In I Chronicles 16:8-36 and II Chronicles 6:40-42 we find quotations from Psalms 96; 105; 106; 130; and 132. Solomon's prayer in II Chronicles 6:41 f. is a paraphrase of Psalm 132:8-10. Two of Jesus' words on the cross are from Psalms 22:1 (Mark 15:34; Matthew 27:46) and 31:5 (Luke 23:46). Psalm 18 appears in II Samuel 22 with only very minor alterations.

175   How important is all this?

For the Bible student who is trying to find the deep spiritual messages of the psalms these historical and literary details are of little importance. Such matters are probably of interest only to the literary or historical student. For the devout reader who is interested in getting at the great truths in the psalms it is necessary to approach them from an entirely different angle.

176   How should devout students approach them?

They should know something of the original purposes for which the psalms were composed, something of the circumstances to which they refer, and something of the divine truths they contain—if any. When one knows the place they filled in the life of the ancient Jew, one is better prepared to understand the message they may contain. On this basis, and for this purpose, we will divide the book of Psalms into two great groups.

177   What are those two groupings?

1. Those designed for use in public worship in the Temple.
2. Those designed for private devotions, or for the training of the personal religious life of the individual.

178   Of what did the Temple worship consist?

The modern student may find it difficult to appreciate the great place in the life of the Jew which was filled by the Temple. In the first place, the building itself was the most gorgeous structure in the city of Jerusalem in the years following the Exile. There has been a tendency to exaggerate the magnificence of Solomon's Temple. It was a great building, and very impressive, of course; but, as we have already learned, it was much less imposing than the royal palace and several of the other public buildings. But when the city was destroyed in 586 B.C. by the Babylonians, all these great structures went up in flames, and the Temple was the only one that was ever rebuilt. Thus it stood out in solitary grandeur in the year 400 B.C., when Ezra proclaimed the Book of the Law.

In addition to the pre-eminence of the Temple as a building, it was central in the affection and devotion of the people. It enjoyed a reverence that was accorded to no other structure anywhere in the world. In it the Jews believed Yahweh actually lived. It was his home and his divine throne. From it he went forth to exercise authority over the world. At its altars he received the penitent and forgave their sins according to the acceptability of their sacrifices. It was not that the Temple was merely a building wherein the people worshiped; they believed that in the Temple they actually entered into the presence of God.

In connection with the sacred esteem in which the Temple was held by the people, certain feasts, services, and ceremonies were arranged for the Temple, to be performed before its altars. Here hymns were sung, anthems were chanted, the choirs rendered their special psalms, and the people joined in prayers, praises, and devotional exercises, all of which were supposed to please Yahweh and, at the same time, provide the people with an opportunity for the expression of their own joy; for it must always be remembered that there was a very great deal of joy in the life of the people which was associated with their religion.

179 What was the source of this joy?

First of all, they were confident that they had been especially favored at the hands of Yahweh in having been entrusted with the Law. The possession of the sacred covenant was a source of common satisfaction to them. The devout members of the nation treated it with profound reverence and respect, but it was also the source of an overflowing joy for them.

In the second place, being sure that Yahweh lived in the Temple, they found a sense of inner assurance and joy in the belief that they actually stood within his presence when they stood inside the Temple. This made their journeys to the Temple occasions of enthusiastic and hilarious joy. Many of the most exuberant psalms were songs sung by crowds of pilgrims as they neared Jerusalem on their way to perform religious rites in the Temple.

In the third place, they were altogether convinced that the various ceremonies and sacrifices at the altars of the Temple were absolute guarantees of the favor of Yahweh. The sin offering, for instance, was a ceremony concerning the effectiveness of which there was no doubt in the minds of the people. One who offered a proper sacrifice on the altars of the Temple, and accompanied it with the prescribed prayers, went out of the place absolutely sure that one's spiritual accounts were all squared.

180 What was the form of these services?

The modern Protestant Christian, accustomed to thinking of a worship service that includes a sermon, some scripture, prayers, and responses, finds it difficult to think of any other type of service. But among the Jews, and at the Temple altars, the worship service followed a very different form. There was no sermon, though on occasions there seems to have been some sort of address to the people. Choirs about the altars sang chants while the sacrificial animals were slain and while they lay burning upon the altars. In some cases the people sang chants or hymns, or joined in antiphonal responses. By the year 250 B.C., at least, musical instruments were used to augment the singing of the choirs and congregations. Organized on a grand scale, and using hundreds and even thousands of voices, some of these services with their vivid symbolism must have been extremely impressive. The clouds of smoke, the stench of burning flesh, and the oppressive odor of strong incense must have left a deep impression upon the minds of the worshipers, especially those were able to visit the Temple only on rare occasions. It was all very moving and very primitive, but it had in it something of the deep spiritual vitality which made Israel's religion so rugged.

181 How many such services were there?

There were, of course, the regular services on the Sabbath. Then each day there were certain sacrifices and ceremonies. But the great occasions were the annual feasts, of which there were three. At such times the people were expected to go up to Jerusalem, if possible, and there join with other pilgrims in the Temple services and celebrations. These were occasions of hilarious joy and were marked with great festivities, so much so that the spirit of rejoicing spread over the land. From the moment that the watchmen cried, "Arise, and let us go up to Zion, to Yahweh our God!" (Jeremiah 31:6), until the weary pilgrims departed from the holy city, it was an experience of uninterrupted pleasure and spiritual satisfaction. Small wonder that the pious Jew exclaimed, "I was glad when they said to me,

'Let us go to the house of Yahweh!'" (Psalm 122:1). The happy throngs converging upon Jerusalem from all directions, marching to the music of bands (Isaiah 30:29) and singing pilgrim songs as they journeyed, must have been a thrilling sight. At least some of these marching songs have been preserved for us in the Pilgrim Psalter.

182   What is the Pilgrim Psalter?

It is a collection of fifteen psalms (120–134) which are believed to have been sung by the Temple pilgrims as they made their way to Jerusalem. It is not likely that they were in every case composed for such pilgrims; but, having a form and theme adapted to such a purpose, they were appropriated by the imulate an exalted spiritual mood among the hosts who filled the highways, sung as they were in something of the style of the Negro spirituals.

183   With what subjects did they deal?

The limited space at our disposal does not permit us to make a detailed study of each psalm, yet we will undertake to find a brief explanation of the main idea back of each of the Pilgrim psalms. But first we should know something of their general form.

184   What was that general form?

There are variations, of course, between the different psalms, but they all follow a general style, best illustrated by Psalm 124. In this case a solo voice took up the theme, "If it had not been Yahweh who was on our side . . ." One can almost hear the high, sustained tone of the singer who prolonged certain syllables to the full limit of their tonal value. Then, according to instructions in the psalm—"let Israel now say" (124:1)—the multitude took up the response. Some scholars believe the solo voice sang each couplet and that the people repeated them through the next eight lines.

> If it had not been Yahweh who was on our side,
>   When men rose up against us,
> then they would have swallowed us up alive,
>   when their anger was kindled against us;
> then the flood would have swept us away,
>   the torrent would have gone over us;
> then over us would have gone
>   the raging waters.

At this point the mighty chorus burst forth in a volume of song praising Yahweh for his watchful care and solicitude:

> Blessed be Yahweh,
>   who has not given us
>   as prey to their teeth!
> We have escaped as a bird
>   from the snare of the fowlers;
> the snare is broken,
>   and we have escaped!
> Our help is in the name of Yahweh,
>   who made heaven and earth.

Thus by solos, antiphonals, responses, and choruses the people sang themselves into an enthusiasm that was both reverent and hilarious. But to study the matter more closely, we will make a brief examination of each psalm in the Pilgrim Psalter.

185 What is the theme of Psalm 120?

This psalm bears the title "A Song of Ascents," as do all the psalms in the Pilgrim Psalter. This means that it is one of the songs sung by the people as they went up to the city of Jerusalem for the religious festivals. In this psalm we have pilgrims who have come a long distance through many dangers. At times they have lost their way and been buffeted by storms. Liars gave them wrong directions, robbers kept them in constant peril, but God delivered them. It is a song of faith in the midst of danger.

186 What is the theme of Psalm 121?

This seems to have been a song sung by the people as they came in sight of the holy city of Jerusalem. The solo voice takes up the song, as already described, singing the first distich:

> I lift up my eyes to the hills.
>   From whence does my help come?

From that point on the host takes up the song in a mighty tide of tone which expresses their abiding faith in Yahweh's help:

> My help comes from Yahweh,
>   who made heaven and earth.

187 What is the theme of Psalm 122?

This lovely psalm is used to this day by any Russian pilgrims who are able to make the journey to Jerusalem, having been a favorite of theirs in the old days. The devout Jew is reminded of the painful career of the holy city and prays earnestly for its prosperity. The description of terror in the hymn suggests that it may have been written sometime during the days of Nehemiah (444 B.C.), but that cannot be known certainly. At any rate it is a song of joy as the pilgrims find themselves, at last, standing inside the sacred precincts.

188 What is the theme of Psalm 123?

This seems to be another psalm in which the solo voice takes up the song:

> To thee I lift up my eyes,
> O thou who art enthroned in the heavens!

Then follows the response of the crowd. The reader will note that the singular pronoun is used in the first verse and plural pronouns thereafter. This indicates that the first verse is a solo and the later verses are for the chorus. The people have their eyes fixed on Yahweh, ready to obey at the first suggestion of his command, in order that they may obtain his mercy. The sense of guilt is acute, and there is an earnest plea for divine forbearance.

189 What is the theme of Psalm 125?

Dr. W. A. Shelton, in the *Abingdon Bible Commentary*, gives a description of the circumstances which provided the background for this brief psalm. He says,

We are to imagine bands of pilgrims crossing the river at Jericho and conducted up to Jerusalem by the Levites, and as they go up they sing of their adventures on the way. They have arrived on the Mount of Olives, or Mount Scopus, their eager eyes catch the first vision of the holy city, they utter a cry of admiration, and then fall to describing it and comparing it to the character of a faithful Israelite. Mountains ever played a great part in Israel's history—Sinai, Hor, Nebo, Olives, Ebal, Gerizim, Carmel, Gilboa, Tabor, Hermon, and Mount Zion, this last the most sacred of all. Mount Zion was the very center and symbol of Israel's religion and of her indissoluble solidarity. To it every devout Jew away from home looked when he prayed and to it each hoped some day to make a pilgrimage. What emotions must have stirred their hearts when first they came to look down upon the holy city from loftier heights, or when they gazed upon the mountains surrounding the hills upon which Jerusalem was situated![3]

---

[3] P. 588. Used by permission of the publisher, Abingdon Press.

190   What is the theme of Psalm 126?

This is a psalm which describes the joy of the first returning exiles. Even their neighbors have been impressed with the things Yahweh has done for them. The present, however, is discouraging (v. 4). There is a drouth on, and the people are in want, and the psalm closes with an earnest prayer that the restoration may be completed (vv. 5-6).

191   What is the theme of Psalm 127?

Someone has called this psalm the "Hebrew's 'Cotter's Saturday Night.'" All good and useful things, it declares, come from Yahweh—he is the source of all benefits, and nothing prospers without his blessing, the most strenuous efforts without his assistance being wasted. The second half of the psalm (vv. 3-5) declares that a father's greatest joys are in his children.

192   What is the theme of Psalm 128?

The home life of the Jew has always been one of the conspicuous virtues of the race, and this psalm presents a picture of the family circle in which the fear of the Lord is the guiding principle. This holy spirit of devotion may be counted upon to save the nation.

193   What is the theme of Psalm 129?

The long history of the nation has been filled with tragedy, but it has survived through the help of Yahweh. Whatever success its enemies may have is temporary. This has been true in the past and certainly will be true in the days to come. It is easy to imagine the pilgrims singing this psalm as they plod down the highway, en route to Jerusalem. Very naturally they would review their nation's past and consider its precarious present, but their profound faith comes to their rescue, and this ancient psalm provides an expression somewhat as the modern Christian might sing, "O God, our help in ages past, our hope for years to come."

194   What is the theme of Psalm 130?

Sometime, perhaps during the days of Nehemiah, a devout

Jew composed a psalm of penitence in which sins were confessed in the most contrite terms. "If thou didst keep strict tally of sins," Dr. Moffatt translates the line, "O Lord, who could live on?" Because it so perfectly expressed the penitence of the pilgrims who were coming up to Jerusalem to offer their sacrifices, they adopted it, and it found its way into the Pilgrim Psalter. It was probably a prayer poem in more or less common use throughout the nation when the Pilgrim Psalter was being compiled.

195 What is the theme of Psalm 131?

The ancient prophets had made extravagant promises to the people concerning the restored nation—promises which had not been fulfilled. There were those among the people who had lost heart, and without discussing those promises this psalm expresses confidence in Yahweh and declares that the psalmist will be satisfied with whatever he may send. It ends with an exhortation to the people to put their confidence in Yahweh.

196 What is the theme of Psalm 132?

There have been dark days in the past. There was, for instance, that period in David's reign when the ark had no resting place and the nation was surrounded with enemies, yet Yahweh had delivered the nation. Similar provision for the nation's needs may be expected now. This psalm seems to be made up of speeches by several individuals, and may have been composed for a group. Verses 1 and 2 are reminders of David's preparations for the building of the Temple. Verses 3-5 describe his oath; verses 6-7 describe the cooperation the people gave; and verses 8-10 petition Yahweh to bless these efforts and dwell in the sanctuary. This is followed by Yahweh's reply, in which he assures the people that he will bless them and restore the fortunes of David's house.

197 What is the theme of Psalm 133?

This brief little poem extols the beauties of humankindness, and when sung by the pilgrims must have had an extremely wholesome effect. It would be difficult for contentions and strife to develop in the midst of people singing such a song.

198   What is the theme of Psalm 134?

This psalm closes the Pilgrim Psalter and is, in effect, a doxology. It is the song of the pilgrims who are leaving the Temple for the night, and as they go out they exhort the Levites who are to remain in the holy edifice to praise God. The Levites respond with a benediction upon the worshipers, praying Yahweh's blessings upon them as they set out upon their journey to their homes. With a little imagination readers can fancy themselves among the pilgrims just outside the Temple, listening to the choir singing within,

> May Yahweh bless you from Zion,
> he who made heaven and earth!

199   What are we to conclude about the Pilgrim Psalter?

All the psalms contained in the Pilgrim Psalter are designed to strengthen the faith of the people. There are songs from the highways expressive of the devotion of the people, poems that have been born of everyday experiences with the throb of life in them and the dust of the road upon them. They represent the profound faith of the people, and though there may be little formal theology about them, they represent the basic thinking of the people. They are religious folk songs which reveal the fundamental faith of Israel and express the love of the plain people for the Temple, Jerusalem, and Yahweh himself. In studying them, however, we must distinguish them from the processional hymns, several of which are to be found in the book of the Psalms.

200   What are the processional hymns?

The great love of the Jew for Jerusalem and its Temple is expressed in numerous psalms, but nowhere more vividly or beautifully than in Psalm 137:5-6. One must have some appreciation of this great affection to understand the meaning of the services of the Temple and the psalms associated with those services. The great festivals began, for instance, with processional hymns sung at the foot of the Temple hill by the worshipers. The hymns prepared their hearts for the Temple service before ever they entered its sacred portals. Psalm 100 is one such, in which the choir calls upon everyone everywhere to join the song and come with the people as they enter the Temple gates with thanksgiving and praise. It is probable that the last two lines of the psalm were taken up by all the people and sung as a mighty chorus. Serving the same purpose but used somewhat differently is Psalm 95. In this case the people instead of the choir sang the hymn as they approached the Temple. Let readers close their eyes and try to imagine a great multitude of people assembled at the foot of the hill upon which the Temple stood. Let us remember that they are, in large numbers, pilgrims who have made long journeys to be able to stand in the house of Yahweh and in the presence of the Most High.

201 Are there other processional hymns?

There are Psalm 118 and Psalm 24, the latter being used to celebrate victories. Some believe that the latter was used when the sacred ark was carried as a symbol of triumph. A brief hymn opened the ceremony (vv. 1-2); and as the multitude started to ascend the hill to the Temple, a choir sang out the question:

> Who shall ascend the hill of Yahweh?
> And who shall stand in his holy place?

To this the priests—or it may have been a solo voice—responded, describing the kind of people who might enter, those who were moral and upright. At the Temple gate the multitude broke forth into song:

> Lift up your heads, O gates!
> and be lifted up, O ancient doors!
> that the King of glory may come in.

From the Temple a solo voice sang out:

> Who is the King of glory?

and the worshipers answered:

> Yahweh, strong and mighty,
> Yahweh, mighty in battle.

Solos and responses continue to the close of the psalm in what must have been a stirring antiphony. Let the devout recreate the scene if they would get the beauty of these matchless lines and the majesty of the message. Once inside the Temple, however, the actual ceremonies begin. The psalm has nothing to do with the alar ritual; it is altogether preliminary.

202 What about Psalm 118?

This is also a processional hymn, more elaborate and involved than the others. As in Psalm 24, the procession starts at the foot of the Temple hill (v. 1); and, as will be noted (vv. 2-4), the psalm contains instructions to various groups to sing the refrain, "His steadfast love endures for ever" ("Let Israel say," etc.). First Israel is to join the chorus, then the house of Aaron, and then "those who fear Yahweh," and one can almost hear the various groups joining the swelling chorus. As they march up the hill, the song recites the bitter experiences out of which Yahweh has saved the nation. When they arrive at the Temple, a solo voice calls to the Levites to open the gates (v. 19), and they respond (v. 20). They enter singing (vv. 21-25) and are welcomed by a choir of priests (v. 26), who instruct them in the ceremony (v. 27), whereupon they march about the altar (v. 28) touching the sacred horns and singing rhythmically, ending with the final chorus.

203 Were hymns used only as processionals?

By no means. A number were designed to be used in connection with various feasts, probably being sung inside the Temple, before the altars, or in connection with the sacrificial ceremonies. Psalm 81, for instance, was probably used in connection with the Feast of the Passover. The student will notice that there is an exalted moral and ethical note in many of these psalms, which is evidence of the fact that the vigorous teachings of such prophets as Amos, Isaiah, Micah, and Jeremiah had taken deep root in the thinking of the people. Even the priests—so different from those of Amos' day—pleaded with the people in behalf of justice and morality. One could imagine Amaziah, the high priest in charge of the shrine at Bethel who drove Amos from the city, standing in amazement under the sound of such teachings from the lips of Jerusalem priests. For these latter priests seemed to recognize the fact that ritual and ceremony do not suffice, and that any ceremony at the altar, to be effective, must be performed by one whose heart is "pure." This is a great advance over the eighth century and represents the contribution made to the national religion by the prophets. The prophets won even though they did not live to see their triumph. Something of this is also to be found in the thanksgiving hymns.

204 What were the thanksgiving hymns?

The spirit of thanksgiving is to be found in many psalms, but at least two were composed as special prayers to be offered on the occasion of the great national festivals of harvest (65; 67). In Psalm 65 there is an expression of the belief that, though Yahweh is the God of Israel, he is the "hope of all the ends of the earth, and of the farthest seas." This universalism is the beginning of the missionary impulse, even though it is only a rudimentary expression. Here again is the influence of the great prophets. In Psalm 67 there is some of the same spirit of universalism. Yahweh is recognized as the giver of all good gifts—of the increase of the land and the flocks—and as such is worthy to receive the praises and worship of the people. Surely the heathen must recognize him for the wonderful God he is.

205 Were any psalms used in the regular services?

There is Psalm 148, which is a mighty summons to all the earth, and all creatures, to praise Yahweh. Even the planets, the sun, and the moon are invited to join the praise. Then there are a few nature hymns which are an adoration of creation (8), a description of a majestic storm (29), or an appreciation of the wonders of nature (19:1-6). Then there are psalms which deal with Yahweh's interest in national affairs (such as 33; 135; 136), which are in praise of God's great work in history. Psalm 46 celebrates God's interference in behalf of the people in some great crisis. It is said that from this hymn Martin Luther got his inspiration to write "A mighty fortress is our God." Three victory hymns are included in the collection (68; 99; 149). In the case of Psalm 99 we have an unusual form in which the call to praise comes at the end of the stanzas, instead of at the first as is usually the case. It is a very impressive psalm, which praises Yahweh as the mighty God who loves justice, rules the earth in equity, and loves humanity as a gracious and forgiving God. The response, "Holy is he," was sung by the people at the close of each stanza and must have been very impressive. Let the student conjure up the scene with the aid of imagination. Thousands are gathered about the altar and inside the Temple court. A choir of priests sing their praises in a dignified and measured chant, the people listening intently. As they rise to the crescendo,

> Let them praise thy great and terrible name,

the people join in a mighty response,

> HOLY IS HE!

Three times this happens. Thousands take up the words, and each time the volume of tone becomes greater, until the cumulative effect must have been tremendous.

206 Did the Jews really love Yahweh?

The New Testament emphasis upon the ceremonialism of the Jews has had the effect of blinding Christians to the deep basic piety which was at the foundation of Jewish religion. Once we work our way through our preconceptions, however, it is evident that the Jews did entertain an abiding love for Yahweh. Certainly this fact is apparent in numerous psalms. Their tone is unmistakable—the Jews *loved* their God.

207 What about these psalms of love?

There is Psalm 113, which voices praise of Yahweh because of his righteous rule over them, a rule that has evoked their love. He is portrayed as the friend of the humble; and when the Jews sang this psalm at the great annual feasts, it was an expression of their confidence that sometime Yahweh was going to lift up that humble little nation and make it glorious before all the world, because he was righteous, and because the nation had suffered. Of course they were well aware that Yahweh's reign was not yet fully established, but they sang of a fervent hope.

208 Which are the songs of hope?

Psalm 47 is one. Israel, together with the rest of humanity, will witness Yahweh's ascent to his throne as the King of the earth. It is a great vision put into a great psalm. Psalm 96 reflects much of the mood of Second Isaiah as it describes Israel as a missionary and calls the earth's nations to their salvation. Psalm 98 expresses much the same theme. In a somewhat different mood, but still similar in their opinions concerning "the last times" are Psalms 75; 76; 93; 97. In the judgment of many, these seven are the finest in the book so far as poetic and literary style is concerned.

209 Are all the psalms joyful?

The element of joy is conspicuous in the book of Psalms, but it is inevitable that anxiety should obtrude from time to time. There are lamentations and prayers for help. The two great seasons of sorrow for the Jews could not have failed to produce their songs.

210 What were those two seasons?

The first was the period of discouragement soon after the exiles' return from Babylonia. The bitter struggle which ensued, with the reluctant soil, poverty, unfriendly neighbors, insufficient labor, and desolation, left an indelible mark upon the literature of the nation. The second period of sorrow was those years when the people suffered so terribly under the Seleucid kings who undertook to uproot the religion of Yahweh and substitute Greek culture and religion. Known as the Maccabean age, this was perhaps the most tragic and terrible era through which the Jews ever passed, at least within the limits of Bible times.

211 Which psalms came out of these periods?

Reference has already been made to Psalm 126 (Question 190), which reflects the discouragement that overtook the exiles upon their return from Babylonia. Psalm 123 also voices an appeal for deliverance (Question 188). Psalm 85, which seems to have been sung in the Temple service, makes a fervent appeal that Yahweh's indignation shall be turned aside and that he shall show his people kindness. The great and popular Ninetieth Psalm reflects some of the conditions just described and could have come out of either period. It is infinitely sad, and in spite of the fact that it is widely used at funeral services it contains no word about immortality. In spite of the difficulty of dating the psalms, it appears that there are at least five that came out of the Maccabean age.

212 What are the Maccabean psalms?

About the year 170 B.C. Antiochus Epiphanes, the Greek

overlord of the Jews, determined to uproot everything Hebrew and implant Greek culture, religion, philosophy, language, and manners in its place. During this period thousands of devout souls suffered martyrdom, the Temple was desecrated by having swine flesh burned upon its altars, and the most brutal indignities were heaped upon the people. In their extremity the people turned to Yahweh for help, and Psalms 44; 60; 74; 79; 83 (all in Books II and III) voice the terror of those years. Psalm 79 is especially explicit in describing the conditions we have noted—"they have defiled thy holy temple, . . . laid Jerusalem in ruins, . . . given the bodies of thy servants to the birds of the air for food, . . . laid waste his habitation," etc. Psalm 44 (vv. 17-22) stoutly declares Israel's innocence and calls upon Yahweh to bestir himself in behalf of his people.

213 Are no kings mentioned in the psalms?

There are so-called "royal" psalms in the book, which were composed for certain state occasions, such as weddings, coronations, etc.; but they cannot be assigned to any particular king and may not have been designed for such originally, but were perhaps written to express an ideal situation. Psalm 72 is one of the royal psalms, and in the opinion of literary critics is one of the most beautiful in all the book, voicing as it does the prayers of the people in behalf of a new king. Psalm 20 is a prayer in behalf of a king on the eve of battle, and Psalm 21 is a song of thanksgiving when he returns victorious. In Psalms 61; 89; 132; 144 we have other prayers in behalf of kings which give evidence of the place the rulers held in the esteem and affection of their Jewish subjects.

214 What about the private psalms?

There are many psalms in the book which were composed for the benefit of private worshipers, though of course the public worship hymns could be used by individuals in their private devotions. But of these personal hymns there are two groups: (1) those psalms used in private worship in the Temple, and (2) those to be used in worship outside.

215 What was the private worship in the Temple?

So much attention has been given to the public services of worship in the Temple that the average person is apt to lose sight of the fact that much private worship was conducted there also. This was due to the very nature of the Temple and the place it occupied in the religious life of the people. To the Temple they went to pray in behalf of their private business ventures, their family affairs, and other personal matters. To the Temple they brought their sin offerings; there they paid their vows, solemnized their oaths, and paid their tithes. The Temple itself became much more than a religious building. It served also in something of the function of a bank, a courthouse, a legislative hall, and a historical library.

Since the Temple stood at the very heart of the life of the nation, it was perfectly natural that individuals should have come to it for private devotions. Just as many modern people drop in on their church for a season of quiet prayer, so the devout Jew turned to the Temple. Also, as the modern Catholic goes to the church for confession and for the assurance of the forgiveness of sins, so the ancient Jews turned to the altars in the Temple and offered sacrifices by which they believed they were assured of forgiveness.

216 What were these sacrifices?

Usually they were animals without blemish—bullocks, sheep, oxen—but in the case of the very poor, in Jesus' day, it was permitted that they should offer two pigeons. The animal was killed in a prescribed manner; the blood was allowed to drain off in a particular fashion; and the carcass was "burned" upon the altar. Each move in the process had a spiritual significance, and the entire ceremony was invested with a very grave seriousness.

217 What psalms were used in connection with such sacrifices?

Psalm 66 is a song of thanksgiving which was probably used in connection with such a private service. The Temple choir began with a hymn (vv. 1-4). Then one section sang vv. 5-7, and another sang vv. 8-12. At this point the individual worshiper stepped forward and sang:

> I will come into thy house with burnt offerings;
>   I will pay thee my vows,
> that which my lips uttered
>   and my mouth promised when I was in trouble.

69

I will offer to thee burnt offerings of fatlings,
    with the smoke of the sacrifice of rams;
I will make an offering of bulls and goats.

Thereupon the worshiper turned to whatever company was assembled and sang a personal testimony, which completed the psalm.

In a few cases it appears that psalms were used in connection with cases that had come into the courts.

218 What about the songs in cases before the courts?

There were occasions when people took refuge in the Temple when pursued by their enemies or accused of crime. In some instances they came to the Temple to seek vindication of charges that had been laid against them. Psalm 26 seems to have been a song sung by a man who was trying to clear himself from some terrible accusation. The charge is not specified, but the law required that one clear oneself by an oath (Exodus 22:8, 11), and this is the idea that underlies the psalm. The psalmist stoutly denies his guilt and calls upon Yahweh to hear his defense (vv. 1-5). Following his denial of guilt he washes his hands in a rite which symbolizes complete cleanness (v. 6). This done, the priest absolves him of the charge, and he begins a sacred dance about the altar, which concludes with a solemn vow that he will continue to live an upright life. The psalm moves on an exalted plane with a fine spirit of dignity unlike the bitter imprecatory psalms.

219 What about the bitter psalms?

Among the scholars they are known as the "imprecatory" psalms, and from a spiritual viewpoint they represent the lowest point in the Old Testament. Psalm 5 is the prayer of a devout man who is praying in the Temple in the morning. He is well aware that wicked persons are not permitted inside the Temple (see Psalm 15) and offers thanks for the privilege of worshiping there. Then his prayer takes a bitter turn, in which he accuses his enemies of violence and fervently pleads that Yahweh visit severe judgment upon them. Psalm 109 is the most bitter of all, containing some awful curses, yet it was used as a psalm of worship—which will suggest something of the estimate in which worship was held by the people. Many of the psalms voice the complaint that the psalmists have been deserted by their friends, that disease has overtaken them, that suffering has overwhelmed them, and that their strength is ebbing away (Psalms 38:11; 41:5-9; 71:10 ff.). But for the most part the psalmists accept their troubles as a deserved punishment for their private sins and freely confess their own evil (38:1, 4, 18).

220 What about the psalms in private worship outside the Temple?

To appreciate these psalms it is necessary that we take a hurried look back over the spiritual history of the Jews. It will be remembered that in Amos', Isaiah's, and Micah's day Jews seldom prayed for themselves as individuals. Their prayers, for the most part, were offered in behalf of the nation. Religion did not become personal until Jeremiah's time. That great prophet of the last days in Jerusalem taught the people that God did deal with the individual. But with the nation destroyed, the Temple in ruins, and Jerusalem a mass of rubble, the religious life of the exiles took a new direction. The personal element began to assume more significance. Ezekiel and Second Isaiah contributed very largely to this mood. During the exile the sense of individual responsibility began to develop. Individuals began to pray for themselves as well as for the nation. By the time Ezra arrived on the scene with the Book of the Law and the new emphasis on personal responsibility, the whole trend of religion was taking a new direction, and this had the effect of producing a number of psalms which were strictly individual in character.

221 What is the form of these individual psalms?

Some are private prayers; some are songs of thanksgiving; but all of them express moods, emotions, ideals, and aspirations of a soul that is alone with God. Their chief characteristic is their complete independence of the whole altar-sacrificial system. Occasionally we find a psalmist in actual revolt against the system (51:16). Psalm 40 (v. 6) disclaims the value of ritual and ceremony and places the emphasis on obedience to the will and purposes of God. Psalm 50 suggests that all zeal for ritual and sacrifice rests on a mistaken concept of Yahweh (50:8-15). The inner spirit of the worshiper constitutes the real offering (50:23). Psalm 141 declares that right attitudes are better than sacrifices and incense (141:2). The outstanding example of these personal psalms is the 103rd, where the soul enters into a direct and personal communion with Yahweh in an intimacy and beauty that is not surpassed anywhere in the Old Testament. Some of the personal psalms are so significant that we can afford to take a more careful look at them, as the 139th.

222 What about Psalm 139?

This is a study of the nature and character of Yahweh. Its chief concern is his presence everywhere in the universe, and his universal knowledge. It stands alone in the book of Psalms in the fact that it is one of the most thoughtful bits of writing we have coming out of the ancient Jewish world. The poet is overwhelmed by the amazing wonder of the mighty God who is not bound by space or time, and in an abandon of adoration sings this hymn, utterly unable to understand how any person could fail to worship Yahweh or wickedly defy him. The poet hates Yahweh's enemies as though they were the poet's own (139:19-22).

223 Can we name another of the personal psalms?

Psalm 91 is a meditation on the subject of the kindly care and providential interest which God shows in humans. Persons who put their trust in Yahweh will not be subject to the anxieties and cares which others may suffer. They may be sure they will be cared for and may therefore live free from the anxieties which are common among the ungodly. Psalm 101 is a vigorous assertion by someone of power that authority will be administered in a manner which favors the just and punishes the wicked. Psalm 58 expects righteousness to be established by some form of divine intervention, rather than by any effort on the part of humans. Psalm 82 pictures Yahweh as calling the judges and rulers of the earth to an accounting for their administration. Their moral stupidity has threatened the very foundations of the earth, and unless Yahweh helps there will be no help. Psalm 15 describes those who will find favor in the sight of Yahweh and puts the whole matter on the basis of righteousness. In no other way can one placate God or secure his benefits.

The longing of the human soul for relationship with the

divine is a universal experience, and every religion has taken some account of it. Among the Jews it found expression in several psalms which are extremely intimate and tender. There was, for instance, the poet who sang Psalms 42–43 while surrounded by enemies and beset by multiplied dangers, and who instinctively reached out for assurance of God's friendship. On the other hand, the psalmist who gave us Psalm 32 was overjoyed with the assurance that all sins were forgiven, and the song reflects that sense of relief. The justly famous Twenty-third Psalm is, of course, the best-loved of all the Psalter for the simple reason that it expresses this personal faith in the simple and beautiful terms of a shepherd's experience. It is a true picture of the soul that puts its trust in God. And, it must be remembered, all these exalted concepts of life and faith were achieved by those who lived "under the Law."

224   What about this emphasis upon the Law?

The modern Christian is apt to think of the Law as a stiff, mechanical, bigoted, and somewhat petty system. Some of the ceremonies prescribed were no better than that. But it is also true that those who "kept the Law" did, in numerous instances, come into a rich and rewarding spiritual experience. If we compare the Jewish Law with the religious teachings and philosophy of other peoples of the time, it immediately appears infinitely finer and better than any other religious system then known. The modern Christian believes that in Jesus we have the complete and satisfactory revelation of God. But we do him no honor when we declare that the Law under which his ancestors lived had no value. If those growing up under the Law could achieve such a religious experience as that enjoyed by the authors of the twenty-third and thirty-second psalms, then there must have been much good and great vitality in it in spite of its limitations.

We know of a certainty that the Law was held in great affection by high-minded and intensely spiritual Jews. They regarded it much as modern Christians esteem their Bible; they heaped their praises upon it and bestowed their affections upon it. To it they turned in the hours of their extremity, and in it they found the help and encouragement that all the spiritually minded seek.

225   What did the psalmists say about the Law?

There are two psalms which have as their theme the beauty and glory of the Law—19 and 119. The former is a little broader in its interests than the latter. It uses six different terms or phrases as designations of the Law, and makes at least one very impressive statement—"The law of Yahweh is perfect. . . . The precepts of Yahweh are right" (vv. 7-8).

The 119th Psalm is a great acrostic poem and, as such, is a wooden and mechanical composition. This is almost inevitable as a consequence of the plan by which it is put together. But in spite of its restricted literary style, the psalm is an extravagant eulogy of the Law and an appreciation of its spiritual benefits, indicative of the high esteem in which it was held by the devout. Modern Christians may think of the ancient Law as an uninspiring legal system, but those who lived under it seem to have found great blessings thereby, and their praises are extravagant and unrestrained.

226   What about the theology of psalms?

The 150 poems of this collection, written by at least one hundred authors, and having passed through the hands of many editors and compilers before they found their way into the book of Psalms, would inevitably and very naturally express a wide variety of religious convictions. We must keep in mind the fact that we are not studying the opinions and beliefs of one person, even an inspired individual, when we inquire into the teachings of the psalms. Rather we are studying a cross section of Jewish religious opinion as it took form through perhaps three hundred years. Just as one person has one political opinion at one period of history and another person in another period has another opinion, so the religious emphasis of the Jews shifted from age to age, and as a consequence the theology of the psalms differs. But in the main it may be said that the book of Psalms represents the thinking of the Jews on religious matters as they thought about 200 B.C. It was about that time that the book began to take its final form—some few psalms may have been added subsequently—and it is natural to think that the compilers of the collection would not have included any which flatly contradicted their convictions. Therefore the theology of the book of Psalms can be said to represent the general outlines of Jewish thought about God and life as it would have been expressed about 200 B.C. We have already examined their opinion concerning the Law. At least four other matters should be looked at briefly, at least.

227 What four questions remain to be studied?

1. What do the psalmists teach about God?
2. What do they teach about immortality?
3. What do they teach about the moral order?
4. What do they teach about the proper way to serve God?

228 What do the psalmists teach about God?

Their first conviction was that he was *personal*. They found it impossible to think of Yahweh as an abstract principle. Instead they thought of him as one who thinks, loves, and passes moral judgments, is subject to many of the same questions and emotions as those which move us, labors among humans, and is always present in the affairs of the nations.

Their second conviction was that he was *powerful* and perfectly capable of executing any judgment he might reach. The nations of the earth were all subject to him, and no nation could hope to defy him permanently with any success.

Their third conviction was that he *could be appealed to,* that he would listen to people's cries for help, that he coveted their friendship and cooperation, and that he took delight in their love and loyalty. He might be august, majestic, and high above the earth, yet he could always be reached by their appeals.

Their fourth conviction was that through the Law and through personal righteousness on their part, Yahweh *could be persuaded* to do the things they desired, within the limits of righteousness, of course. In other words, he could be influenced to exert his awful powers in their behalf because he had a natural affection for humankind.

229 What do the psalmists teach about immortality?

It is a very interesting and significant fact that there is comparatively little discussion of the subject of immortality in all the Old Testament. Those occasional references which we find usually come from writings which were late in taking form, for it appears that Jewish thinking upon this subject did not develop until later years. There is no word upon this subject in the writings of Amos, Isaiah, Micah, Nahum, Habakkuk, or even Jeremiah. But in at least two places in the psalms there is some mention (Psalms 16; 30:3), though in neither case do we have any thorough discussion of the subject. The author of Psalm 16 is willing to leave the matter to God. The writer does not pretend to know anything about the subject, with a trust so complete that ignorance is immaterial. Not knowing the answer, the author is willing to leave the whole question to Yahweh, trusting him implicitly.

230 What do the psalmists teach about the moral order?

This is the age-old question concerning the moral government of the world. Is it good or bad? Is it friendly or unfriendly toward us? Is there anything in life worth living for? What is the good life? These matters have been examined with care by the author of Job, and in some part by the author of Ecclesiastes. The prosperity of the wicked, the sufferings of the righteous, the slow arrival of justice, and other similar problems have all been weighed with care. At least one of the psalms (37) faces this problem and arrives at the conclusion that we might well beware, for our sins will ultimately catch up with us. It is a reassertion of the old doctrine of retribution with which the prophets had wrestled. The author of Psalm 73, on the other hand, almost lost faith at one time because the facts of life are so contradictory. That author has almost come to the conclusion that it does not pay to strive for righteousness (73:13); but faith reasserts itself before the writer closes the psalm, professing to see the ultimate destruction of the works of wickedness, and calls upon the readers to await Yahweh's vindication with patience (73:18 f.). Yet even this answer is not completely satisfactory, and he proceeds to declare that the only solution thus far found is communion with Yahweh (73:23-28). It is not a satisfactory answer, but faith must go out ahead of reason many times, and the just do live by faith. It is this element of trust and faith which marks the psalms as being the high-water mark of Jewish religious literature (27:1; 23; 46; 73:25).

231 What do the psalmists teach about the proper way to serve God?

The priests and professional prophets of Isaiah's day insisted that the one way to please God was by performing rituals and ceremonies in the proper manner. Jeremiah revolted against this idea, saying that Moses in the wilderness laid no such grievous requirements upon the people (Jeremiah 7:22). In Jesus' day great stress was laid on the proper ways to observe the Sabbath and on cleansings and sacrifices. But the psalms are singularly free from all this. Instead, the psalmists seem to be very much under the influence of the prophets, and insist upon righteous conduct, upright living, and moral character. With all their devotion to the Law, the Temple, and the established institutions of religion, they are singularly free from any slavish dependence upon rites and ceremonies for their spiritual confidence. They think of Yahweh as dwelling in the heavens (2; 7; 11; 18; 29; 33; 57; 68; 76; 92; 93; 96; 102; 103; 115; 123; 136; 144; 150) and judging humans with moral judgments coupled with mercy (36; 92; 103; 107; 111; 113; 117; 118; 136; 145). There are psalmists who actually question the religious values of the Temple rituals (40:1-12), but others think of the Temple as the earthly abode of Yahweh (9; 48; 80; 99; 135). All in all, the spiritual quality of the religion of the psalmists is very high, and for that reason the Psalter has become the source of strength for modern Christians as perhaps no other portion of the Old Testament.

232 What kind of God do we find in the Psalter?

In answering this question we can do no better than quote Dr. Elmer A. Leslie, writing in the *Abingdon Bible Commentary:*

Taking the psalms as a whole, they contain the conception of a majestic God. He is the Creator of the world. The heavens, the sun, the moon, and stars owe their being to him. Man too came to be through God's creative purpose. He is the summit of creation, made "but little lower than God." This whole area of creation is under the Creator's dominion. Nature reveals the very mind of God. The heavens declare his glory. The thunder is his voice. The recurring succession of the seasons, the passing of day into night, the mysterious productivity of the soil, the deep-seated, instinctive processes of animal life—all utter the mind of God. He is all-powerful. He is all-knowing. He is everywhere present.

Moreover, this majestic God is the God of history. All human history moves toward a goal, the reign of God over all mankind, in all the earth. But this ultimate purpose of God is not viewed as achieved through the initiative and effort of men so much as through the direct effort and energy of God. To a unique degree this God of human history is the God of Israel's history. He created Israel and made himself known to her. He is the God of Moses and the Exodus, of Sinai and the wilderness, of the invasion and settlement of Canaan. And this God of Israel is the one sole God of the whole world, who uses Israel to reveal him to the far ends of the earth—a thought common also to the prophets.[4]

233   How should we read the psalms?

Read them as you would read any other religious literature, for the deep spiritual message they will bring to your own soul. Read for considerable lengths of time. Steep the mind in their exquisite language, their exalted moods, their penitence and calm confidence. Read them with an open mind, allowing the inspired words to leap out of the page with particular meaning for particular occasions. Read them for the light they will throw upon the problems of the soul, not for the illumination they will bring to the mind. They came from the hearts of honest and devoted people; bring honesty and devotion to them, and they will reply in kind.

---

[4]P. 514. Used by permission of the publisher, Abingdon Press.